Be prepared...
To learn...
To succeed...

Get **REA**dy. It all starts here. REA's preparation for the PSSA is **fully aligned** with Pennsylvania's Assessment Anchors.

Visit us online at
www.rea.com

READY, SET, GO!®

Pennsylvania

PSSA

8th Grade Reading and Writing

2nd Edition

Staff of Research & Education Association

Research & Education Association
Visit our website at
www.rea.com

The assessment anchors presented in this book were created and implemented by the Pennsylvania Department of Education (PDE). For further information, visit the PDE website at *www.pde.state.pa.us*.

"Space Colonization" photo (p. 61) courtesy NASA.

"Margaret Murie" photo (p. 171) by Associated Press.

Research & Education Association

61 Ethel Road West

Piscataway, New Jersey 08854

E-mail: info@rea.com

Ready, Set, Go!°

PSSA–8th Grade Reading and Writing

Printed in the United States of America

Library of Congress Control Number 2008929861

ISBN 13: 978-0-7386-0482-4

ISBN 10: 0-7386-0482-8

TABLE OF CONTENTS

PART 1: READING

PART 2: WRITING AND REVISING

About Research & Education Association

Founded in 1959, Research & Education Association is dedicated to publishing the finest and most effective educational materials—including software, study guides, and test preps—for students in middle school, high school, college, graduate school, and beyond. Today, REA's wide-ranging catalog is a leading resource for teachers, students, and professionals.

We invite you to visit us at *www.rea.com* to find out how "REA is making the world smarter."

Acknowledgments

We would like to thank Larry B. Kling, Vice President, Editorial, for his editorial direction; Pam Weston, Vice President, Publishing, for setting the quality standards for production integrity and managing the publication to completion; Michael Reynolds, Managing Editor, for project management; Diane Goldschmidt, Associate Editor, for post-production quality assurance; Christine Saul, Senior Graphic Artist, for cover design; Jeremy Rech, Graphic Artist, for interior page design; Jeff LoBalbo, Senior Graphic Artist, for post-production file mapping; and Caragraphics for typesetting this edition.

SUCCEEDING ON THE PSSA: 8ᵗʰ Grade READING AND WRITING

ABOUT THIS BOOK

This book provides excellent preparation for the Pennsylvania System of School Assessment (PSSA) for 8th Grade Reading and Writing. Inside you will find lessons, drills, strategies, and test practice—all of it with a single-minded focus: success on the PSSA.

We have also made every effort to make the book easy to read and navigate.

This book is divided into several parts. The first section is a **PRETEST,** which is half the length of an actual PSSA test and introduces students to some elements of the actual test, including

- Nonfiction reading passages, including biographies and articles

- Fiction reading passages, such as poems and excerpts from novels

- Multiple-choice and open-response questions

Following the pretest is **a lesson section,** which teaches students about the different types of test questions, step by step. A full-length **POSTTEST,** which matches the content and structure of the actual PSSA, appears at the end of the book. An answer key with detailed explanations of each answer is provided.

HOW TO USE THIS BOOK

FOR STUDENTS: To make getting through the book as easy as possible, we've included icons shown on the next page that highlight sections like lessons, questions, and answers. You'll find that our practice tests are very much like the actual PSSA you'll encounter on test day. The best way to prepare for a test is to practice, so we've included drills with answers throughout the book, and our two practice tests include detailed answers.

FOR PARENTS: Pennsylvania has created grade-appropriate Assessment Anchors that are listed in the table in this introduction. Students need to meet these standards as measured by the PSSA. Our book will help your child review for the test and prepare for the exams. It includes review sections, drills, and two practice tests complete with explanations to help your child focus on the areas he or she needs to work on to help master the test.

FOR TEACHERS: No doubt, you are already familiar with the PSSA and its format. Begin by assigning students the pretest. An answer key and detailed explanations follow the pretest. Then work through each of the lessons in succession. When students have completed the subject review, they should move on to the posttest. Answers and answer explanations follow the posttest.

ICONS EXPLAINED

Icons make navigating through the book easier by highlighting sections like lessons, questions, and answers as explained below:

 Question

 Lesson

 Answer

 Activity

 Tip

 Writing Task

WHY STUDENTS ARE REQUIRED TO TAKE THE PSSA

In 1999 Pennsylvania adopted academic standards for several subjects, including Reading and Writing. To determine how well a student is advancing and whether the student is on course to perform well in high school, eighth grade students are required to take the PSSA.

It is one of the key tools used to identify students who need additional instruction to master the knowledge and skills detailed in the Assessment Anchors, which guide education in Pennsylvania.

WHAT'S ON THE PSSA

Reading

The reading portion of the PSSA is divided into three sections, which are placed in between three sections of mathematics. The reading sections contain fiction or nonfiction passages, followed by multiple-choice questions. In some cases, students must answer open-ended questions, which means they must write out their answers instead of selecting from a list of possible answers.

The breakdown of the reading sections on the PSSA is as follows:

Section Breakdown

Reading Section 1: Passages followed by 24 multiple-choice questions and 2 open-ended questions

Reading Section 2: Passages followed by 16 multiple-choice questions and 2 open-ended questions

Reading Section 3: Passages followed by 16 multiple-choice questions and 2 open-ended questions

Writing

The writing portion of the PSSA contains both passages with embedded errors and multiple-choice items, and writing prompts for which students must write out their answers in an essay. Students will complete two sessions of multiple-choice items first, and then they will respond to both an informational and persuasive writing prompt.

ASSESSMENT ANCHORS*

The multiple-choice and open-ended questions on the PSSA are based on the following Assessment Anchors:

READING
Fiction

		Page Numbers
R8.A.1.1	Identify and apply the meaning of vocabulary.	35
R8.A.1.2	Identify and apply word recognition skills.	35
R8.A.1.3	Make inferences, draw conclusions, and make generalizations based on text.	53
R8.A.1.4	Identify and explain main ideas and relevant details.	71
R8.A.1.5	Summarize a fictional text as a whole.	71
R8.A.1.6	Identify, describe, and analyze genre of text.	88

*The assessment anchors presented in this table were created and implemented by the Pennsylvania Department of Education (PDE). For further information, visit the PDE website at *www.pde.state.pa.us.*

Nonfiction

R8.A.2.1	Identify and apply the meaning of vocabulary in nonfiction.	36
R8.A.2.2	Identify and apply word recognition skills.	36
R8.A.2.3	Make inferences, draw conclusions, and make generalizations based on text.	53
R8.B.3.1	Interpret, describe, and analyze the characteristics and uses of facts and opinions in nonfictional text.	53
R8.B.3.2	Distinguish between essential and nonessential information within or between texts.	53
R8.B.3.3	Identify, compare, explain, interpret, describe, and analyze how text organization clarifies meaning of nonfictional text.	53
R8.A.2.4	Identify and explain main ideas and relevant details.	71
R8.A.2.5	Summarize a nonfictional text as a whole.	71
R8.A.2.6	Identify, describe, and analyze genre of text.	88

Both fiction and nonfiction

R8.B.1.1	Interpret, compare, describe, analyze, and evaluate components of fiction and literary nonfiction. (includes questions about character, plot, setting, theme, and content)	105
R8.B.1.2	Make connections between texts.	105
R8.B.2.1	Identify, interpret, describe, and analyze figurative language in fiction and nonfiction.	122
R8.B.2.2	Identify, interpret, describe, and analyze the point of view of the narrator in fictional and nonfictional text.	122

WRITING

TIPS FOR THE STUDENT

Students can do plenty of things before and during the actual test to improve their test-taking performance. The good thing is that most of the tips described in the following pages are easy!

Preparing for the Test

Test Anxiety

Do you get nervous when your teacher talks about taking a test? A certain amount of anxiety is normal and it actually may help you prepare better for the test by getting you motivated. But too much anxiety is a bad thing and may keep you from properly preparing for the test. Here are some things to consider that may help relieve test anxiety:

- Share how you are feeling with your parents and your teachers. They may have ways of helping you deal with how you are feeling.

- Keep on top of your game. Are you behind in your homework and class assignments? A lot of your classwork-related anxiety and stress will simply go away if you keep up with your homework assignments and classwork. And then you can focus on the test with a clearer mind.

- Relax. Take a deep breath or two. You should do this especially if you get anxious while taking the test.

Study Tips & Taking the Test

- **Learn the Test's Format.** Don't be surprised. By taking a practice test ahead of time you'll know what the test looks like, how much time you will have, how many questions there are, and what kinds of questions are going to appear on it. Knowing ahead of time is much better than being surprised.

- **Read the Entire Question.** Pay attention to what kind of answer a question or word problem is looking for. Reread the question if it does not make sense to you, and try to note the parts of the question needed for figuring out the right answer.

- **Read All the Answers.** On a multiple-choice test, the right answer could also be the last answer. You won't know unless you read all the possible answers to a question.

- **It's Not a Guessing Game.** If you don't know the answer to a question, don't make an uneducated guess. And don't randomly pick just any answer either. As you read over each possible answer to a question, note any answers that are obviously wrong. Each obviously wrong answer you identify and eliminate greatly improves your chances at selecting the right answer.

- **Don't Get Stuck on Questions.** Don't spend too much time on any one question. Doing this takes away time from the other questions. Work on the easier questions first. Skip the really hard questions and come back to them if there is still enough time.

- **Accuracy Counts.** Make sure you record your answer in the correct space on your answer sheet. Fixing mistakes only takes time away from you.

- **Finished Early?** Use this time wisely and double-check your answers.

Sound Advice for Test Day

The Night Before. Getting a good night's rest keeps your mind sharp and focused for the test.

The Morning of the Test. Have a good breakfast. Dress in comfortable clothes. Keep in mind that you don't want to be too hot or too cold while taking the test. Get to school on time. Give yourself time to gather your thoughts and calm down before the test begins.

Three Steps for Taking the Test

1) **READ.** Read the entire question and then read all the possible answers.

2) **ANSWER.** Answer the easier questions first and then go back to the more difficult questions.

3) **DOUBLE-CHECK.** Go back and check your work if time permits.

TIPS FOR PARENTS

- Encourage your child to take responsibility for homework and class assignments. Help your child create a study schedule. Mark the test's date on a family calendar as a reminder for both of you.

- Talk to your child's teachers. Ask them for progress reports on an ongoing basis.

- Commend your child's study and test successes. Praise your child for successfully following a study schedule, for doing homework, and for any work done well.

- Talk about test anxiety. Your child may experience nervousness or anxiety about the test. You may even be anxious, too. Here are some helpful tips on dealing with a child's test anxiety:

  - Talk about the test openly and positively with your child. An ongoing dialogue not only can relieve your child's anxieties but also serves as a progress report of how your child feels about the test.

  - Form realistic expectations of your child's testing abilities.

  - Be a "Test Cheerleader." Your encouragement to do his or her best on the test can alleviate your child's test anxiety.

PRETEST

READING

Section 1

Read the passages in this section and then answer the questions. You will have 45 minutes to complete this section. Mark your multiple-choice answers on the answer sheet provided at the end of this test.

Read the following excerpt about a poor young boy who dreams of being a prince.

The Prince and the Pauper

An Excerpt
by Mark Twain

London was fifteen hundred years old, and was a great town—for that day. It had a hundred thousand inhabitants—some think double as many. The streets were very narrow, and crooked, and dirty, especially in the part where Tom Canty lived, which was not far from London Bridge. The houses were of wood, with the second story projecting over the first, and the third sticking its elbows out beyond the second. The higher the houses grew, the broader they grew. They were skeletons of strong criss-cross beams, with solid material between, coated with plaster. The beams were painted red or blue or black, according to the owner's taste, and this gave the houses a very picturesque look. The windows were small, glazed with little diamond-shaped panes, and they opened outward, on hinges, like doors.

The house which Tom's father lived in was up a foul little pocket called Offal Court, out of Pudding Lane. It was small, decayed, and rickety, but it was packed full of wretchedly poor families. Canty's tribe occupied a room on the third floor. The mother and father had a sort of bedstead in the corner; but Tom, his grandmother, and his two sisters, Bet and Nan, were not <u>restricted</u>—they had all the floor to themselves, and might sleep where they chose. There were the remains of a blanket or two, and some bundles of ancient and dirty straw,

but these could not rightly be called beds, for they were not organised; they were kicked into a general pile, mornings, and selections made from the mass at night, for service. . . .

No, Tom's life went along well enough, especially in summer. He only begged just enough to save himself, for the laws against mendicancy[1] were stringent, and the penalties heavy; so he put in a good deal of his time listening to good Father Andrew's charming old tales and legends about giants and fairies, dwarfs and genii, and enchanted castles, and gorgeous kings and princes. His head grew to be full of these wonderful things, and many a night as he lay in the dark on his scant and offensive straw, tired, hungry, and smarting from a thrashing, he unleashed his imagination and soon forgot his aches and pains in delicious picturings to himself of the charmed life of a petted prince in a regal palace . . .

He often read the priest's old books and got him to explain and enlarge upon them. His dreamings and readings worked certain changes in him, by-and-by. His dream-people were so fine that he grew to lament his shabby clothing and his dirt, and to wish to be clean and better clad. He went on playing in the mud just the same, and enjoying it, too; but, instead of splashing around in the Thames solely for the fun of it, he began to find an added value in it because of the washings and cleansings it afforded . . .

By-and-by Tom's reading and dreaming about princely life wrought such a strong effect upon him that he began to ACT the prince, unconsciously. His speech and manners became curiously ceremonious and courtly, to the vast admiration and amusement of his intimates. But Tom's influence among these young people began to grow now, day by day; and in time he came to be looked up to, by them, with a sort of wondering awe, as a superior being. He seemed to know so much! and he could do and say such marvellous things! and withal, he was so deep and wise! Tom's remarks, and Tom's performances, were reported by the boys to their elders; and these, also, presently began to discuss Tom Canty, and to regard him as a most gifted and extraordinary creature. Full-grown people brought their perplexities to Tom for solution, and were often astonished at the wit and wisdom of his decisions. In fact he was to become a hero to all who knew him except his own family—these, only, saw nothing in him.

[1]**mendicancy:** begging

1. Why did Tom like to swim in the Thames?

   A to have fun

   B to get clean

   C to drink water

   D to move about

2. As used in the passage, what does the word
   <u>restricted</u> mean?

   A moved

   B limited

   C rejected

   D punished

3. Which word best describes Tom?

   A hopeful

   B successful

   C imaginative

   D disappointed

4. This passage is mainly about a boy dealing
   with problems caused by

   A location

   B jealousy

   C a lack of care

   D a lack of money

5. Which of the following is a metaphor?

   A ". . . and they opened outward, like
   doors."

   B "They were skeletons of criss-cross
   beams. . ."

   C "His head grew to be full of these
   wonderful things . . ."

   D "The streets were very narrow, and
   crooked, and dirty . . ."

6. Based on their descriptions and their actions, how can Tom's family be described? Use two examples from the passage to support your answer.

Read the following passage about Chinese Immigration to Angel Island, a registration center in California.

Chinese Immigration to Angel Island

In the 1800s and 1900s, immigrants flocked to America to escape poverty and oppression and enjoy a better life in "the land of the free." Most of these immigrants were processed, or registered, at an immigration center on Ellis Island in New York City, but those entering the country through California were processed at an immigration center on Angel Island in the San Francisco Bay. Many of these immigrants were from China.

The immigration stations on Ellis and Angel Islands differed in that Angel Island was actually a detention center. While immigrants processed on Ellis Island waited hours or days to enter America, those processed on Angel Island were forced to wait weeks or months. A shortage of jobs in the West and racial prejudice were to blame. A series of discriminatory laws were passed that made it difficult for Asians to enter the United States. The Chinese were the most seriously affected by these laws.

Many Chinese initially immigrated to America in search of gold in California, which they nicknamed the "Gold Mountain." They were soon to uncover the fallacy of the "Gold Mountain," however, as they were met with resentment and suspicion from Americans and forced to work menial jobs for little pay. These first immigrants laid railroad tracks, reclaimed swamp land, worked as migrant farmers, and labored in the fishing and mining industries. While they toiled away for long hours under treacherous working conditions, many still remained optimistic about the future

and were grateful to be in America, where they were free.

When the American economy faltered in the 1870s, the situation became even more serious for the Chinese. Because the Chinese were willing to work for extremely low wages, Americans living in the West felt that they were the reason for the lack of employment. They passed laws that were even more restrictive, and some Chinese who were already settled in America were cruelly deported to <u>impoverished</u> imperial China. According to these new laws, only persons born in the United States or whose husbands or fathers were U.S. citizens were allowed to enter or remain in the country. Desperate to remain in America, some Chinese managed to falsify "papers" stating that they had fathers who were citizens of the United States.

These Chinese were called "paper sons" and "paper daughters." However, this falsification of papers led to an even longer detainment for Chinese trying to enter America—a few were detained for years! They were asked ridiculous questions by interrogators looking for a reason to deport them. Wrote one Chinese detainee:

I told myself that going by this way would be
*   easy.*
Who was to know that I would be imprisoned at
*   Devil's Pass?*
How was anyone to know that my dwelling place
*   would be a prison?*

A new detention center opened on Angel Island in 1910, and its location, which was even more isolated than the first, was considered ideal for interrogations. This new center had space for more detainees and regular boat service to the mainland. Over the next thirty years, 175,000 Chinese immigrants were detained there. To express their feelings of loneliness and fear of brutality and deportation, some detainees carved poetry into the wooden walls of the detention center, some of which is still visible today. Wrote one detainee:

America has power, but not justice.
In prison, we were victimized as if we were guilty.
Given no opportunity to explain, it was really
*   brutal.*

Despite being mistreated, the Chinese permitted to live in America made great contributions to their new country. They supplied labor to American factories, especially during the Civil War when laborers were in short supply. Some Chinese-American entrepreneurs started their own businesses, which sparked the American economy. Using their advanced agricultural knowledge, Chinese-Americans in the West converted what was once useless land into rich farming soil, making the West self-sufficient and no longer dependent upon the East for food. Chinese immigrants brought with them their language, beautiful writing, culture, and customs, which were eventually integrated into American society.

The United States abandoned the detention center on Angel Island in 1940, when "Chinese Exclusion Acts" were repealed and a fire destroyed the administration building. A museum has been established in the old detention center, so visitors can see what life was like for these early Americans. The Angel Island Immigration Station Foundation (AIISF), a non-profit group of concerned individuals and descendants of Chinese-Americans once detained on Angel Island, hopes to preserve and restore the immigration station, which they consider an important part of American history.

7. Why does the author quote lines from poetry carved into the walls of the detention center on Angel Island?

   A to show how the Chinese felt about their detainment

   B to emphasize that the Chinese were there a long time

   C to prove that the Chinese on Angel Island were mistreated

   D to show that the Chinese detained on Angel Island were artistic

8. Which best describes the organization pattern in this passage?

   A cause and effect

   B in order or sequence

   C compare and contrast

   D in order of importance

9. As used in the passage, what does <u>impoverished</u> mean?

   A poor

   B distant

   C dangerous

   D populated

10. Why do people today consider the Angel Island registration center important?

   A It is a popular tourist attraction.

   B It is an important part of American history.

   C It proves that the Chinese were treated unfairly.

   D It shows the contributions of the Chinese in America.

11. It is likely that the creators of the second detention center on Angel Island intended to

   A process more Chinese

   B detain and deport more Chinese

   C assist more Chinese entering America

   D discourage Chinese from entering the country

12. The main purpose of this passage is to

   A entertain readers with stories about immigrants on Angel Island

   B persuade people to visit Angel Island and learn about its history

   C provide readers with information about the Chinese on Angel Island

   D describe what it was like for the Chinese made to stay on Angel Island

Read this passage about Sojourner Truth, a black woman who fought for equal rights.

Sojourner Truth: Traveling Preacher

From its beginning, Isabella Baumfree's life was shrouded in hardship. She was denied freedom, separated from her parents, and treated like other people's property. Nobody could have imagined that, years later, she would assume the role of a powerful leader under the name Sojourner Truth.

In 1797, before slavery was abolished in the northern states of America, Baumfree was born into slavery in New York. Since her parents were slaves, she was forced to inherit that horrible destiny. As a young woman she was taken from her family and auctioned to different owners.

One of her owners arranged for her to marry another slave, named Thomas, and together they had five children. These children were in turn considered slaves, and most were taken away and sold just as Isabella and her siblings had been. Isabella could no longer <u>tolerate</u> the suffering. She snatched up her smallest child, abandoned Thomas, and escaped her enslavement.

In 1827, shortly after her escape, the state of New York emancipated its slaves. Isabella, Thomas, and all of their children were finally free. However, that announcement did little to alleviate their troubles. To earn a living, Isabella had to become a house servant for the Van Wagenen family. She even used their name temporarily. During her employment with the Wagenens, Isabella discovered that one of her previous owners had illegally sold her son to a slaveholder in Alabama. She recognized the crime that had been committed and courageously chose to bring the case to court. The

I Sell the Shadow to Support the Substance.
SOJOURNER TRUTH.

court ruled in her favor and forced the crooked slave owners to release her son.

This was Isabella's first taste of empowerment. She had defended her cause successfully. Now she was determined to spread that power to other black people and women who, at the time, had very little power to speak of.

Isabella was an ideal leader. She was about six feet tall, an exceptional height for a man or woman in her day. She also had developed muscular arms and shoulders from hundreds of days spent plowing fields. Her voice was remarkably deep, but she tempered it with her beautiful singing. Although she was illiterate, she was intelligent, humorous, and well-spoken.

She found additional motivation in religion, joining various communes and movements and studying their beliefs. In 1843, she renamed herself Sojourner Truth. A sojourner is a temporary resident; with her new name, she announced her new role as a traveling preacher.

Soon, Sojourner Truth had become famous for her speeches on women's rights and anti-slavery topics. Her most well-known speech is remembered for its dominant challenge: "Ain't I a Woman?" She delivered this speech in 1851 at the Women's Convention in Akron, Ohio. In it, she linked the plight of black people in the south with the plight of white women in the north, and called for change. This is part of what Sojourner told her audience:

"That man over there says that women need to be helped into carriages, and lifted over ditches, and to have the best place everywhere. Nobody ever helps me into carriages, or over mud puddles, or gives me any best place—and ain't I a woman? Look at me. Look at my arm! I have plowed and planted, and gathered into barns, and no man could head me—and ain't I a woman? I could work as much and eat as much as a man, when I could get it, and bear the lash as well—and ain't I a woman? I have borne thirteen children, and seen most all sold off to slavery, and when I cried out with my mother's grief, none but Jesus heard me—and ain't I a woman?"

While Sojourner was extremely intelligent, she always expressed herself in a straightforward manner. She concluded her legendary speech by simply saying, "Obliged to you for hearing me, and now old Sojourner ain't got nothing more to say."

The start of the Civil War in 1861 brought many of Sojourner's major concerns to the forefront. However, while the slavery question was being settled on battlefields across the nation, she was planning for life after the war.

By the time Sojourner Truth died in 1883, her contributions had given Americans many new ideas for the future. She was definitely a person ahead of her time. Sojourner spoke out for women's suffrage (voting rights) approximately 70 years before women gained the legal right to vote. She supported the temperance movement, which urged the government to put restrictions on alcohol, at least 50 years before the government decided to attempt it. She even personally challenged Abraham Lincoln to end segregation on street cars in 1864—which was 91 years before Rosa Parks sparked the modern civil rights movement by refusing to give up her seat on a city bus to a white person.

13. As used in this passage, what does the word <u>tolerate</u> mean?

    A forbid

    B understand

    C put up with

    D look at

14. The main purpose of this passage is to

    A describe the history of slavery in America

    B tell readers about an important event in history

    C inform readers about the life of a brave woman

    D convince people to fight for what they believe in

15. What does the phrase "first taste of empowerment" mean in the fifth paragraph?

    A She felt powerful for the first time.

    B She realized things would soon change.

    C She discovered what it was like to be free.

    D She realized she was meant to be in charge.

16. When Soujourner says that "no man could head me," she means that

    A no man could outwork her

    B no man was taller than her

    C no man was as smart as she

    D no man could tell her what to do

17. According to the article, what is a sojourner?

    A a person who sings

    B a temporary resident

    C a born leader

    D a truthful person

Section 2
Read the following passages and answer the questions. You will have 35 minutes to complete this section. Mark your multiple-choice answers on the answer sheet provided at the end of this test.
Read this article about a man who made an amazing discovery.

Digging up James Fort

Archeologist William Kelso had a shovel, a wheelbarrow, and a mission. He was determined to unearth the remains of James Fort, an early British settlement in America. Most archeologists thought he would discover nothing but dirt. They believed that over the centuries the James River had washed away the land on which the fort had once stood. Kelso was in the minority who thought the fort, which he thought of as "an archeological time capsule," could still be found.

Kelso received permission to begin an excavation on the 22-acre island in Virginia where the fort had been constructed in 1607. He commenced digging with his simple tools as local people gathered to observe him. Within hours, Kelso had found more evidence than he'd anticipated. He found metal buttons, armor and weapons, pieces of copper, animal bones, and fragments of dishes,

pots, and pipes. Kelso had located a trash pit—an early kind of dump—of enormous proportions.

When he showed historians what he had found, they were astounded. A group of historians decided to give Kelso funding to continue his excavation. With that money, Kelso was able to hire a team of assistants and purchase better equipment. They found over four hundred thousand artifacts from the colonial years. One of their most important discoveries was not an artifact at all. In fact, to the untrained eye, this discovery looked just like black ink stains on the dirt. But Kelso knew that these stains represented the remains of the wooden walls of the fort. The team knew then that they hadn't just been digging in a nameless old dump. They had actually found the outline of two of James Fort's three walls, totaling two-hundred-and-fifty feet of logs. After uncovering the whole

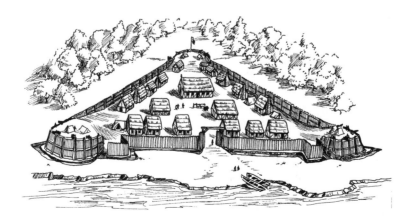

area between the walls, Kelso realized he had located the spot where the American government was first conceived, hundreds of years previously. He was soon to discover evidence, however, that that was not all that happened in James Fort.

The history of James Fort, and the whole area called Jamestown, is a terrible one. Only about one out of six people who moved there from England survived. The colony was characterized by power struggles, massacres, and starvation. Many historians believed that poor planning was the cause of these problems. When British leaders decided to colonize Jamestown, they did not carefully consider what type of citizens should immigrate there. Instead, they mostly sent aristocrats, servants, and craftspeople. Few of these people knew how to grow their own food. The aristocrats were considered lazy and selfish and spent their time arguing over who should be in control of the colony. Furthermore, the British leaders who organized the colony were mostly concerned with finding gold. They encouraged the colonists to search for gold and barter with the Native Americans. "The colony's primary goal was to make a profit for the sponsors," Kelso wrote. This greedy goal left the colonists little time to improve their own community.

Kelso's discoveries contradicted some popular beliefs about what had happened in Jamestown. He discovered that the people of James Fort were not lazy. They had many tools that they used for their everyday tasks. Scattered around the fort and the trash pits were bullet molds, metal-working tools, glass-making tools, animal bones, weapons, fishhooks, and oyster shells. Researchers concluded that the colonists had hunted, fished, and made useful crafts.

Kelso's team also found lots of metal, especially copper, at the site. In the 1600s, the British had hoped that Native Americans would be impressed with metal tools and ornaments, since most Native Americans relied on tools made of stone and wood. The Jamestown colonists expected to be able to trade copper to the natives for food and gold. However, some British sailors secretly sold copper directly to the Native Americans in the area. Because of this, the natives didn't need any more copper and didn't want to trade with the colonists. This was one of the primary factors in the downfall of James Fort.

The colonists continually struggled to find enough food. At first they relied on gifts of corn from nearby Native American villages. However, a severe drought caused most crops to die, and food became scarce all over Virginia; they called this "the starving time." The Native Americans could no longer afford to give food away. The Jamestown colonists were starving and desperate. They began attacking native villages in order to steal food. The natives in turn attacked the colonists, and surrounded James Fort. Trapped inside their fort, hundreds of colonists died of starvation and disease. Kelso's team found a hastily made cemetery full of Jamestown's most unfortunate residents.

The early years of Jamestown were a tragic failure, but they gave many people hopes for new opportunities in America. Jamestown went on to become the first capital of Virginia. Soldiers camped there in the Revolutionary and Civil Wars. Thousands of new colonists immigrated to the area to begin new lives, having learned valuable lessons from the hardships that had taken place in James Fort.

18. The excavation was unusual because it

    A took place on an island

    B was authorized by the government

    C involved digging deep into the ground

    D was started by a single dedicated person

19. With which statement would the author most likely agree?

    A Some historians have inaccurate ideas about the past.

    B Life in Jamestown was difficult but enjoyable.

    C William Kelso should not have investigated James Fort.

    D The colonists did nothing to anger the Native Americans.

20. Which sentence best supports the idea that Kelso's discoveries differed from some popular beliefs about what had happened in Jamestown?

    A "They'd actually found the outline of James Fort."

    B "However, a severe drought caused most crops to die."

    C "The Jamestown colonists were starving and desperate."

    D "He found out that the people of James Fort were not lazy."

21. What is the main idea of this article?

    A Many factors contributed to the death of the first people in Jamestown.

    B People in Jamestown eventually entered into conflict with Native Americans.

    C William Kelso made a discovery that helped people learn about life in Jamestown.

    D William Kelso discovered artifacts that proved people in Jamestown hunted and fished.

22. What was Kelso's most important discovery at Jamestown?

    A fishhooks

    B animal bones

    C working tools

    D wooden walls

23. How did William Kelso use his findings to learn about the history of Jamestown? Explain two ways in which he used his findings. Use information from the passage to support your answer.

_____

_____

_____

_____

_____

_____

_____

_____

_____

_____

_____

_____

_____

_____

_____

_____

_____

_____

_____

_____

_____

_____

Read the following story about a boy who asks for criticism about a story he has written. Then answer the questions that follow.

Ouch!

Enrico slipped off his jacket and tossed it on the lawn beside him. The bright sun had warmed the chilly morning air. Enrico picked up a marigold and began removing the dirt around its roots before placing it into one of the shallow holes he and his grandfather had dug. "No, no, Enrico, don't do that," his grandfather gently <u>chided</u>. "It's better to leave the root ball intact. If you break off the soil, you might damage the roots and kill the plant."

Enrico smiled and placed the flower in the hole with the roots and surrounding soil intact. His grandfather, his *abuelo*, was a man of great experience and wisdom. He had taught Enrico many things throughout the years. He had taught him the importance of using good-quality lumber while they built a garden shed together in the backyard. Under his grandfather's guidance, Enrico had learned how to make the world's greatest tortillas using peppers so hot they burned your lips. Most of the novels Enrico devoured at night were his grandfather's picks. Grandfather often recommended a new read for Enrico, usually one that was obscure but wonderful, the kind of book you might find at a yard sale rather than a bestseller's list.

Now Enrico wanted his grandfather to teach him how to be a better writer. Even though he had learned English as a second language, Grandfather had become adept enough to publish several history books and had worked for many years as a news reporter for their local paper. "I want to be a writer," Enrico announced as he gently pushed the soil around the marigold so it stood straight in its new home. "I've actually written several short stories. I was hoping you would read them and tell me what you think—and not just tell me that they're good. I want your guidance, so I can improve my writing abilities and become a published writer."

Grandfather shook his head. "Ah, I don't know, Enrico. It isn't easy having your writing critiqued, and I wouldn't want to chance hurting your feelings. You're a bright young man. If you choose to become a writer, you will be a great one, with or without my help."

Despite his grandfather's warnings, however, Enrico finally persuaded him to critique one of his short stories. Enrico selected his best piece: a tale about a boy who was the smallest and worst player on his basketball team. The boy, Miguel, was often teased by the other players for his lack of height and skill. Enrico had revised the story several times until he was certain that his command of the English language was at its best. He printed a copy of the story and left it on his grandfather's kitchen table with a note on top that said, "Tell the truth, Grandfather. I can take it, really I can. And I greatly appreciate your help."

After school the next day Enrico rushed to his grandfather's house. "Did you read it?" He asked as his grandfather rubbed a wet dish with a towel and placed it on a shelf.

"Of course I read it, son," Grandfather said and grinned, "and I think you're a very good writer."

Feeling frustrated, Enrico sighed and plopped in a kitchen chair. This was not what he wanted to hear. "Could you give me more than that?" he asked as he ran his fingers through his hair. "Could you tell me what is good about the story and what is bad? Please?"

Grandfather pulled out a chair and sat down beside Enrico. He picked up the printout of Enrico's story. "You need to show more and tell less, for starters," Grandfather advised. "For example, don't tell the reader that Miguel had a sad look on his face. What about Miguel's face looked sad? Describe his face and let your readers draw their own conclusion." Enrico nodded. "And your plot is so predicable that I knew Miguel was going to score the winning basket after reading only the first paragraph. Why not have him miss the shot, but impress his teammates with his newly acquired skill?"

Enrico frowned. "Ouch!" he exclaimed. "Wasn't there *anything* you liked about my story?" he scoffed.

Grandfather laughed loudly. "I told you it's tough to hear criticism regarding your writing. Writing is a process and, as a writer, your work must undergo many revisions. This is normal, Enrico."

"Maybe I don't have the talent to become a published writer," Enrico confessed, doubting himself.

"You definitely have the talent, but do you have the perseverance? Great writers do not give up. They keep on revising until they get it right."

Enrico smiled. "I hear what you're saying and I won't give up. I'm ready to try again, and I will keep trying until my work is as good as it can be," Enrico said. Grandfather shook his hand. "That's my boy," he said. "I am very proud of you."

24. Which pair of words **best** describes Grandfather?

    A   devious but kind

    B   tough but helpful

    C   mean but honest

    D   impatient but smart

25. What is the main reason Grandfather does not want to read Enrico's story?

    A   He does not think it will be any good.

    B   He does not enjoy suggesting changes.

    C   He does not want to hurt Enrico's feelings.

    D   He does not believe Enrico will listen to him.

26. As it is used in the story, what does the word <u>chided</u> mean?

    A   claimed

    B   corrected

    C   concealed

    D   challenged

27. Which sentence best summarizes what happens in "Ouch!"?

    A   A boy tells his grandfather that he has decided to become a writer.

    B   A boy has learned a great deal from his grandfather over the years.

    C   A boy learns an important lesson about writing from his grandfather.

    D   A boy writes a story about a basketball player who lacks skill and size.

28. What is one problem with Enrico's story?

    A   The outcome is obvious.

    B   The first paragraph is too long.

    C   The main character is ordinary.

    D   The language needs improvement.

WRITING

Directions: This part of the writing test contains two passages with multiple-choice questions. Mark your answers on the answer sheet provided at the end of this test.

Passage 1

Read the passage below and then answer questions 1–4.

Dear Council Members,

1 Banning skateboarding in our town is a bad idea. **2** It is not fair. **3** To the kids who like to ride skateboards. **4** I know lots of people in our town. **5** I have many friends who like to skateboard. **6** These kids are not doing anything wrong. **7** They are simply having fun. **8** And skateboarding is actually a sport. **9** It's not as if these kids are commiting a crime.

10 People say that skateboarders are rude and that they make too much noise. **11** This is not true. **12** My friends are not rude skateboarders and they are actually very quiet. **13** They try very hard to stay out of _____ way and they never damage anyone's property.

14 Skateboarding keeps kids healthy. **15** It is great exercise. **16** So please think about these reasons, because they are important reasons.

Sincerely,

Emily Garcia

---

1. **Which sentence should the writer remove from the passage because it is not relevant to the topic?**

   A sentence 4

   B sentence 5

   C sentence 11

   D sentence 15

2. **Which of the following would work best as the concluding sentence for this passage?**

   A It would be great if skateboarders could voice their feelings about this issue.

   B Skateboarding is safe if kids wear helmets and pads on their knees, and elbows.

   C People should realize that kids are people too and that they have rights.

   D With some careful thought, we can come up with a solution that will make everyone happy.

3. **Choose the correct form of the word to fill in the blank in sentence 13.**

They try very hard to stay out of _____ way and they never damage anyone's property.

A people

B peoples

C people's

D peoples'

4. **Which word is spelled incorrectly?**

A <u>commiting</u> in sentence 9

B <u>noise</u> in sentence 10

C <u>healthy</u> in sentence 14

D <u>exercise</u> in sentence 15

Passage 2

Read the passage below and then answer questions 5–8.

> **1** It is difficult to describe a redwood tree. **2** These trees are so large and beautiful they take your breath away. **3** A redwood tree grows from a seed no bigger than a seed from any other plant. **4** When it is full-grown a redwood tree might be as tall as a skyscraper!
>
> **5** Some redwood trees are very old. **6** If nothing destroys a redwood tree, ___ will live many, many years.
>
> **7** Many redwood trees grow along California's North Coast. **8** The climate there is perfect for redwoods. **9** The air is cool <u>but</u> moist. **10** Redwoods grow well in this environment.

5. **Which sentence shows the correct placement of a comma in sentence 4?**

   A   When, it is full-grown a redwood tree might be as tall as a skyscraper!

   B   When it is, full-grown a redwood tree might be as tall as a skyscraper!

   C   When it is full-grown, a redwood tree might be as tall as a skyscraper!

   D   When it is full-grown a redwood tree, might be as tall as a skyscraper!

6. **Which sentence would best fit after sentence 5?**

   A   Redwoods produce many seeds, which grow into new trees.

   B   A few have been around in the days of the dinosaurs!

   C   Redwoods provide a lot of shade and protect other bushes and trees.

   D   In some places, they are in danger of becoming extinct.

7. **Choose the correct word to fill in the blank in sentence 6.**

   If nothing destroys a redwood tree, ___ will live many, many years.

   A   it

   B   they

   C   them

   D   you

8. In sentence 9, which word <u>best</u> replaces the underlined word?

    A so

    B or

    C and

    D for

PERSUASIVE WRITING PROMPT

You will have up to 60 minutes to plan, write, and proofread your response to this writing prompt.

> To save money to build a new gymnasium, your principal has decided to offer instruction for several classes using distance education, meaning you would only "see" your teacher via a television screen when a videotape is played. Write a letter to the editor of your school newspaper convincing him or her that this is or is not a good idea.

Write your essay on the next three pages.

Plan

Before you write:

- Read the prompt carefully so you understand exactly what you are being asked to do.
- Consider topic, task, and audience.
- Think about what you want to write.
- Use scratch paper to organize your thoughts. Use strategies like mapping or outlining.

Write

As you write:

- Maintain a clear and consistent position or claim.
- Include specific details; use examples and reasons to support your ideas.
- Use a variety of well-constructed, complete sentences.
- Use a logical organization with an obvious introduction, body, and conclusion.

Proofread

After you write:

- ❑ Did you support your ideas with specific details?
- ❑ Do the point of view and tone of the essay remain consistent?
- ❑ Check for capitalization, spelling, sentence structure, punctuation, and usage errors.

USE NO. 2. PENCIL ONLY

**PERSUASIVE WRITING PROMPT
FINAL COPY**

_____

_____

_____

_____

_____

_____

_____

_____

_____

_____

_____

_____

_____

_____

_____

_____

_____

_____

_____

_____

_____

_____

_____

_____

_____

_____

_____

GO ON ➡

USE NO. 2. PENCIL ONLY

**PERSUASIVE WRITING PROMPT
FINAL COPY**

_____

_____

_____

_____

_____

_____

_____

_____

_____

_____

_____

_____

_____

_____

_____

_____

_____

_____

_____

_____

_____

_____

_____

If you need additional space, please continue on the next page.

GO ON

USE NO. 2. PENCIL ONLY

**PERSUASIVE WRITING PROMPT
FINAL COPY**

STOP

MARKING INSTRUCTIONS

Make heavy BLACK marks.
Erase cleanly.
Make no stray marks.

● CORRECT MARK

◉ ⊘ ⊗ ◗ INCORRECT MARK

Multiple-choice questions

1. Ⓐ Ⓑ Ⓒ Ⓓ

2. Ⓐ Ⓑ Ⓒ Ⓓ

3. Ⓐ Ⓑ Ⓒ Ⓓ

4. Ⓐ Ⓑ Ⓒ Ⓓ

5. Ⓐ Ⓑ Ⓒ Ⓓ

6. Ⓐ Ⓑ Ⓒ Ⓓ

7. Ⓐ Ⓑ Ⓒ Ⓓ

8. Ⓐ Ⓑ Ⓒ Ⓓ

9. Ⓐ Ⓑ Ⓒ Ⓓ

10. Ⓐ Ⓑ Ⓒ Ⓓ

11. Ⓐ Ⓑ Ⓒ Ⓓ

12. Ⓐ Ⓑ Ⓒ Ⓓ

13. Ⓐ Ⓑ Ⓒ Ⓓ

14. Ⓐ Ⓑ Ⓒ Ⓓ

15. Ⓐ Ⓑ Ⓒ Ⓓ

16. Ⓐ Ⓑ Ⓒ Ⓓ

17. Ⓐ Ⓑ Ⓒ Ⓓ

18. Ⓐ Ⓑ Ⓒ Ⓓ

19. Ⓐ Ⓑ Ⓒ Ⓓ

20. Ⓐ Ⓑ Ⓒ Ⓓ

21. Ⓐ Ⓑ Ⓒ Ⓓ

22. Ⓐ Ⓑ Ⓒ Ⓓ

23. Ⓐ Ⓑ Ⓒ Ⓓ

24. Ⓐ Ⓑ Ⓒ Ⓓ

25. Ⓐ Ⓑ Ⓒ Ⓓ

26. Ⓐ Ⓑ Ⓒ Ⓓ

27. Ⓐ Ⓑ Ⓒ Ⓓ

28. Ⓐ Ⓑ Ⓒ Ⓓ

Student Name_____

WRITING ANSWER SHEET

MARKING INSTRUCTIONS

Make heavy BLACK marks.
Erase cleanly.
Make no stray marks.

CORRECT MARK   **INCORRECT MARK**

Multiple-choice questions

1. Ⓐ Ⓑ Ⓒ Ⓓ   5. Ⓐ Ⓑ Ⓒ Ⓓ

2. Ⓐ Ⓑ Ⓒ Ⓓ   6. Ⓐ Ⓑ Ⓒ Ⓓ

3. Ⓐ Ⓑ Ⓒ Ⓓ   7. Ⓐ Ⓑ Ⓒ Ⓓ

4. Ⓐ Ⓑ Ⓒ Ⓓ   8. Ⓐ Ⓑ Ⓒ Ⓓ

Student Name_____

Pretest Reading Answers

Section 1

1. **B** A.1.3 (make inferences, draw conclusions, and make generalizations)

   The passage says that Tom swam in the Thames *not* solely for the fun of it but also to wash and cleanse himself. Answer choice B is correct.

2. **B** A.1.1 (identify and apply meaning of vocabulary)

   The passage says that Tom was not restricted because he slept on the floor and could sleep wherever he pleased. Limited is the best answer choice, since he was not limited to sleeping in one place in a bed.

3. **C** B.1.1 (describe and analyze characters)

   Tom is very imaginative. He lives in poverty but dreams of what it would be like to be a prince. He does this so often he begins to act like a prince.

4. **D** A.1.4 (identify and explain main ideas and relevant details)

   While some of Tom's problems may be caused by a lack of care, most are caused by his family's poverty. Therefore, answer choice D is the best answer.

5. **B** B.2.1 (identify figurative language)

   A metaphor compares two things by letting one stand for the other. The houses were not really skeletons; the author compares them to skeletons. Answer choice B is the correct answer.

6. B.1.1 (describe characters)

   Sample answer:

   Tom is dirty and sleeps on the floor. While his family is very poor, they don't seem to care about him. They are given only the remains of a blanket or two to stay warm and these are kicked into a pile in the morning and not treated with much respect. Furthermore, at the end of the story it says that Tom was a hero to all who knew him except his own family. It says that they saw nothing in him. This also supports the idea that they don't care a great deal about him.

7. **A** A.2.6 (identify and/or describe the author's intended purpose of text)

   The author quotes lines from the poetry carved in the wall of the detention center on Angel Island to show how the Chinese felt about being detained. The other answer choices do not closely relate to the information revealed in the quotations.

8. **B** B.3.3 (analyze and explain how text organization clarifies meaning)

   The author tells about the events on Angel Island in the order in which they happened. Answer choice B is the correct answer.

9. **A** A.2.1 (identify meaning of vocabulary)

   The word "impoverished" means poor. Many Chinese left their country because they could not find employment. Therefore, you can tell from the context that imperial China was very poor.

10.   **B**   A.2.3 (make inferences, draw conclusions, and make generalizations)

People today are working hard to restore the registration center on Angel Island because it is part of America's history. By visiting the center, people can more closely imagine and appreciate what early immigrants experienced.

11.   **B**   A.2.3 (make inferences, draw conclusions, and make generalizations)

The second detention center was larger and the author said its creators liked its isolated location, which implies that some Chinese were brutally interrogated in an effort to deport them. Answer choice B is the best answer.

12.   **C**   A.2.6 (identify and/or describe the author's intended purpose of text)

The main purpose of this passage is to inform. It doesn't entertain or convince. Answer choice C is the best answer to this question.

13.   **C**   A.2.1(identify the meaning of vocabulary)

"Tolerate" means "put up with." Answer choice C is the best answer.

14.   **C**   A.2.6 (identify and/or describe the author's intended purpose of text)

The author's main purpose was to inform readers about the life of a brave woman. Answer choice C is the correct answer. While the author does discuss aspects of slavery and fighting for what you believe in, the main focus is on the life of Isabella.

15.   **A**   A.2.1 (apply the meaning of vocabulary)

Isabella's "first taste of empowerment" was the first time she ever felt powerful. Answer choice A is the correct answer. Isabella took the slave owners to court to get her son released from slavery and won her case. It was the first time in her life that the slave owners had to listen to her.

16.   **A**   A.2.3 (make inferences, draw conclusions, and make generalizations)

Sojourner describes the work that she does and then says "no man could head me." You can tell from the context that she means no man could outwork her. Answer choice A is the best answer.

17.   **B**   A.2.4 (identify and explain main ideas and relevant details)

A sojourner is a temporary resident. Answer choice B is the correct answer. According to paragraph 7, Isabella chose the name Sojourner Truth when she decided to become a traveling preacher.

Section 2

18.   **D**   A.2.4 (identify and explain main ideas and relevant details)

The author makes a point to show how the James Fort excavation was unusual because it was initiated, or begun, by a single dedicated archeologist. The opening of the article describes how William Kelso worked alone in the beginning of his impressive task.

19.   **A**   A.2.6 (identify and/or describe the author's intended purpose of text)

The author of this passage would mostly likely agree that some historians have inaccurate ideas about the past. As indicated in the passage, many historians believed that the Jamestown colonists were lazy. In reality, though, they were not lazy.

20. **D** A.2.6 (identify and/or describe the author's intended purpose of text)

The article explains that many historians believed that the tragedies at the Jamestown colony were caused by lazy colonists. However, by excavating the James Fort and finding evidence of hard work, Kelso proved that the colonists had not been as lazy as believed.

21. **C** A.2.4 (identify and explain main ideas and relevant details)

This article contains many ideas, but the main idea is that William Kelso made a discovery that helped people learn about life in Jamestown. In the article, all of the other ideas branch out from this one. Answer choice C is the best answer.

22. **D** A.2.4 (identify and explain main ideas and relevant details)

The article says that the remains of the wooden fort was the most important discovery. Answer choice D is the correct answer.

23. A.2.4 (identify and explain main ideas and relevant details)

Sample Answer: *William Kelso studied his findings in order to learn about Jamestown. The artifacts he found revealed the way people lived then. Objects like fishhooks and animal bones suggested that the people hunted and fished. Tools used for making glass and metal showed that the people created useful crafts. Kelso also learned from things that weren't artifacts, like the stains left in the dirt by the fort's walls.*

24. **B** B.1.1 (describe and analyze character)

The best answer choice is B: Grandfather is tough; he wants Enrico to do his best, but he is also very helpful. Answer choice A is not correct because there is no evidence that Grandfather is devious. Answer choice C is not correct, because Grandfather is not mean to Enrico, and answer choice D is not the best answer because there really isn't any evidence that Grandfather is impatient.

25. **C** A.1.4 (identify and explain main ideas and relevant details)

In the story, Grandfather tells Enrico that he does not want to chance hurting Enrico's feelings. This is why he is reluctant to read the story. None of the other answer choices are supported by the story.

26. **B** A.1.1 (identify and apply the meaning of vocabulary)

When the story says Grandfather gently *chided* Enrico, he has just corrected him. "Claimed" is not the same as "chided"; "concealed" would mean Grandfather has hidden something from Enrico and Grandfather has not challenged Enrico, so answer choice B is the best answer.

27. **C** A.1.5 (summarize a fictional text)

This question asks you to identify the best summary to the story. The summary is what the whole story is about. It is the main message of the story. Answer choice C is the best summary of the story because it states that Enrico learned a lesson about writing. The other answer choices state main ideas.

28. **A** A.1.4 (identify and explain main ideas and relevant details)

Grandfather tells Enrico that he knows what will happen in his story after reading only the first paragraph.

Pretest Writing Answers

1. **A** 1.5.8.E (revise writing after rethinking logic of organization)

   The number of people the author knows in her town is not relevant to the main idea of her letter: that banning skateboarding in her town is unfair.

2. **D** 1.5.8.E (revise writing after rethinking logic of organization and rechecking central idea)

   The best (and most convincing) concluding sentence is to ask for a conclusion that will make everyone happy. Answer choice D is the best answer.

3. **C** 1.5.8.F (edit writing using the conventions of language)

   The word "people" is already plural. (Person is singular.) In this sentence, you need to make it plural possessive. "People's" is the correct answer.

4. **A** 1.5.8.F (edit writing using the conventions of language)

   The word "committing" has two *m*'s and two *t*'s.

5. **C** 1.5.8.F (edit writing using the conventions of language)

   "When it is full-grown" is an introductory clause, which should be followed by a comma.

6. **B** 1.5.8.E (revise writing after rethinking logic of organization and rechecking central idea)

   Sentence 5 mentions that some redwoods are very old and sentence 6 says that some redwoods live many years. Answer choice B best fits in with this idea.

7. **A** 1.5.8.F (edit writing using the conventions of language)

   The pronoun in this sentence refers to "a redwood tree," which is singular. Answer choice A is correct.

8. **C** 1.5.8.F (edit writing using the conventions of language)

   "Cool" and "moist" are related ideas, which should be joined by "and."

   Sample answer:

   To the editor:

   I am writing in response to Principal Snyder's decision to turn certain required classes into distance education classes. I think this is a horrible idea. I understand that the principal is trying to save money to build a new gym, but it seems that he's willing to do so by sacrificing the quality of our education.

   Since when is a videotape a good substitute for a teacher? With no teacher present to monitor students' progress, some students may get bored with the material quickly while others may have trouble keeping up. There will be no one there to gauge when it is appropriate to slow down or move on. What if we have questions about confusing material? If our teacher can only be seen on a videotape, there will be no one present to answer our questions and give us feedback on assignments and tests. There has to be a better way for the school district to save money than by reducing our teachers and classes to videotapes.

   Sincerely,

   Terrell Warner

PART 1: *Reading*

 ## Lesson 1: Word Recognition

Fiction

R8.A.1.1   Identify and apply the meaning of vocabulary.

- Identify and/or apply meaning of multiple-meaning words used in text.

- Identify and/or apply a synonym or antonym of a word used in text.

R8.A.1.2   Identify and apply word recognition skills.

- Identify how the meaning of a word is changed when an affix is added; identify the meaning of a word from the text with an affix.

- Define and/or apply how the meaning of words or phrases changes when using context clues given in explanatory sentences.

Nonfiction

R8.A.2.1   **Identify and apply the meaning of vocabulary in nonfiction.**

- Identify and/or apply meaning of multiple-meaning words in text.

- Identify and/or apply meaning of content-specific words in text.

R8.A.2.2   **Identify and apply word recognition skills.**

- Identify and apply how the meaning of a word is changed when an affix is added; identify and apply the meaning of a word from the text with an affix.

- Define and/or apply how the meaning of words or phrases changes when using context clues given in explanatory sentences.

Word recognition questions

To answer questions about vocabulary, you may have to figure out the meaning of a word from its **context**, or the way it is used in a sentence. You can often find clues to a word's meaning from looking at the surrounding sentences. Sometimes the word might be unfamiliar to you and other times it might be a word with multiple meanings and the question will ask you to choose the correct meaning based on how the word is used in the sentence. You might also be asked to determine the meaning of a phrase. You often need to look at the sentences around the sentence containing the phrase to do this.

Questions for this assessment anchor might also ask you to use the parts of a word—prefixes, roots, and suffixes—to determine a word's meaning. You will also need to identify synonyms or antonyms of words used in the text.

On the PSSA, word recognition questions are asked for both fiction and nonfiction passages. Sometimes a sentence is pulled out from the passage and used in a question, as in "Read this sentence from the passage." Other times, the word is underlined in the passage and you have to go back to the passage to read the sentence containing the word.

Activity

Try to figure out the meaning of these words from the way they are used in each sentence. Look the words up in a dictionary to check your answers.

- With seven siblings and twenty-six cousins, Matt had a *plethora* of relatives.
- All that remained of the small boat was some *flotsam* floating on top of the water.
- Shaking her head, Shelley admitted the location of her missing notebook was an unsolvable *conundrum*.
- Under the *tutelage* of my older sister Miranda, I finally learned to swim.
- Nan, Lil, Bob, and Ava are names that are examples of *palindromes*.

Passage 1

Now read this passage and then answer the questions that follow.

America's First Zoo

The Philadelphia Zoo was the first zoo in America. English settlers came up with the idea for the zoo back in the 1700s. They were very interested in wildlife both in America and other countries. They were intrigued with stories of sailors who returned from foreign lands with animals no one had ever seen before. They wanted to keep these animals in a zoo. They dreamed that children and adults could visit the animals at the zoo and learn all about them. The zoo they imagined was a beautiful place with ponds and parks, where people could enjoy a picnic lunch. Life was <u>arduous</u> for these early settlers, however, and they were never able to make their zoo a reality.

Concrete plans for the Philadelphia Zoo actually began in 1859 when a charter establishing the Zoological Society of Philadelphia was approved and signed. People were very excited. It seemed as if their long-awaited zoo might actually become a reality. But when the Civil War started, it wreaked havoc on America. People feared for their lives and plans for the zoo were put on hold. Philadelphia was unable to open its zoo for another fifteen years!

The Philadelphia Zoo opened its gates on July 1, 1864—and what a day it was! Over three thousand visitors flocked to the zoo from Philadelphia and nearby cities and states. Visitors traveled to the zoo on foot, on streetcars, and in horse-drawn carriages. The zoo even had its own wharf where boats could dock. A steamboat crossing the Schuylkill River dropped off visitors every fifteen minutes! A band played, flags few, and people cheered. Philadelphia welcomed the opening of its zoo—the first zoo in America—with open arms. Admission was only 25 cents per adult and 10 cents per child.

During its first year of operation, the zoo acquired 813 animals and received well over 228,000 visitors. While the Victorian gates, gatehouse, and location of the zoo remain the same, the zoo has grown a great deal over the years. Its attendance is over one million visitors per year!

 Questions

1.   What do you think the word <u>arduous</u> means in this passage?

_____

_____

2.   What does the word <u>concrete</u> mean as it is used here?

_____

_____

3.   The passage says that the Civil War "wreaked havoc" on America and that, because of this, plans for the zoo were put on hold. What does the phrase "wreaked havoc" mean?

_____

_____

Check your answers on the next page.

Passage 1: "America's First Zoo"

 Answers

1. **Sample answer:** <u>Arduous</u> means "difficult." Life for the early settlers was so difficult that they did not have time to make their dream a reality.

2. **Sample answer:** The word <u>concrete</u>, as it is used in this passage, means "definite."

3. **Sample answer:** The phrase "wreaked havoc" means "disrupted." The Civil War disrupted the lives of Americans so much that they could not continue their plans for a zoo.

Passage 2

Read the following passage. When you finish reading, answer the questions that follow.

Catching the Butterflies

A week before the championship basketball game, Jenna developed a sensation of <u>discomfort</u> in her stomach. She wasn't queasy, hungry, or overfull. She didn't know exactly what was causing the sour feeling.

After practice she limped off the court, one hand on her stomach, and mentioned the problem to her coach. The coach said it was probably just a case of pre-game "butterflies." Jenna thought his assessment could not possibly be accurate. Her team was undefeated and Jenna herself was considered their most valuable player. What was there to be nervous about?

Later that day, Jenna visited the school nurse, Ms. Williams. After a quick examination, the nurse concluded that there was nothing physically wrong with her. Ms. Williams looked at Jenna thoughtfully and asked, "Is something causing you stress? Sometimes emotional stress can influence your physical health."

Jenna was convinced that she was not under any stress, and replied, "Nope, everything's just fine with me."

Ms. Williams suggested that she try to relax and not overexert herself, and to report back if her symptoms <u>persisted</u>. Jenna said that she would, and then returned to class. However, she didn't really follow the nurse's advice. She continued training and practicing as hard as ever. Jenna was determined to ignore her stomachache in the hope that it would slip away and not interfere with the big game.

On the morning before the game, Jenna's stomach was tied in a knot. The agitated sensation was so severe that she didn't want to eat all day. Needless to say, by the evening, when her team was gathering for its pep talk, she was hungry and grumpy. When she hit the court, though, she felt a little better. The sound of the crowd and the whoom-boom-boom of the dribbling were soothing. Jenna quickly forgot about her stomach and played as well as she could manage. Her team won the trophy that night, and during the celebrations afterward, she realized she'd completely forgotten about her pain. It was gone.

"It looks as though your stomachache's gone," remarked the coach.

Jenna nodded and smiled, "I think it was just a few butterflies."

 Questions

1. Read this sentence from the story.

    A week before the championship basketball game, Jenna developed a sensation of discomfort in her stomach.

    What does the word <u>discomfort</u> mean?

    A   uneasiness
    B   great pain
    C   confusion
    D   embarrassment

 Tip

Remember that the prefix *dis-* means "not." So Jenna was not comfortable.

2. What does the phrase "hit the court" mean as it used in the sixth paragraph of the passage?

    A   found the court
    B   was on the court
    C   fell on the court
    D   made noise on the court

 Tip

What was Jenna doing when she was on the court? Which answer choice best describes her activity?

3. As it is used in the passage, what does the word <u>persisted</u> mean?

   A   relaxed
   B   stopped
   C   continued
   D   worsened

Tip

The nurse tells Jenna to come back if her symptoms persist. Think about the best answer choice based on this context and eliminate incorrect answer choices.

4. The story says that on the morning before the game, Jenna's stomach was "tied in a knot." What does the phrase "tied in a knot" mean as it is used here?

   _____

   _____

   _____

   _____

Now check your answers on the next page. Read the explanations after each answer.

Passage 2: "Catching the Butterflies"

 Answers

1. A   The word <u>discomfort</u> means "not comfortable." The word <u>uneasiness</u> means almost the same as "not comfortable," so this is the correct answer choice.

2. B   The phrase "hit the court" means that Jenna was actually on the basketball court. Choice B is the correct answer.

3. C   While answer choice D might also seem correct, Jenna would obviously return to the nurse if her symptoms worsened, but the nurse tells her to return if they persist, or continue. Answer choice C is the best answer.

4.   **Sample answer:** When the author says that Jenna's stomach was "tied in a knot," he or she means that Jenna's stomach was really bothering her. She was probably very nervous before the game.

Passage 3

Read the following passage. Then answer the questions at the end of the passage.

The Common Cold: Unbeatable Bug?

While the human race has accomplished many amazing feats, curing the common cold has not been one of them. Even after hundreds of years of research, scientists still cannot stomp out the tiny bug.

Nearly everyone knows the miserable feeling of having a cold. The sickness can affect your entire head with symptoms including sneezing, coughing, a blocked or runny nose, a sore throat, and a headache. Some especially nasty colds carry all these symptoms.

A cold can really disrupt your life. Every year, millions of people miss work or school due to colds. This hurts the economy and the educational system. People spend billions of dollars each year for medicines to reduce their nagging symptoms. So far, no medicine has been proven beyond a doubt to work, however.

The term "cold" is actually just a label for a group of symptoms. These symptoms are actually caused by viruses, microscopic parasites that rely on other organisms to live. When these viruses find a good host—you, for instance—they thrive, but end up giving you some sort of disease in return. Talk about ungrateful guests!

However, in the case of a cold, the disease itself isn't usually what bothers you. The most annoying symptoms are actually caused by your own immune system, which does everything it can to <u>eradicate</u> the virus. The immune system will produce extra mucus to try to flush out the virus through the nose or to trap it and take it to the stomach, where it will be killed with stomach acid. This mucus, of course, results in the cold's most notorious symptom: the runny nose. The stuffy head symptom is caused by inflammation of blood vessels above the nose. Sneezing and coughing are brought about by the irritation caused by the immune system's defense mechanisms. Coughing, in particular, occurs when the irritation moves to the lungs.

Perhaps the only good thing about this cycle of discomfort is that it usually results in success within a week or so. The virus dies and is flushed away, and good health returns. Most people, however, still lament the fact that colds last as long as they do.

Throughout history, people have tried hundreds of different remedies in order to shorten the durations of their cold symptoms. Even powerful leaders like Napoleon Bonaparte concerned themselves with their nasal health. Napoleon had a recipe for cold pills that he claimed worked wonders for him—this recipe included such peculiar ingredients as "ipecacuanha root," "squill root," "gum ammoniac," and "gum arabic." Other old-time recipes called for almonds, currants, poppy seeds, or licorice.

Remedies like these may sound funny today, but we have to be humble because we haven't found a <u>surefire</u> remedy, either. Many scientists today believe that certain kinds of zinc, a substance often used in vitamins, provide our best hope for relief. Chicken soup is always a safe bet, too.

Scientists agree that the best way to avoid the nuisance of a cold is to avoid catching the cold in the first place. Cold viruses are transmitted from person to person. Contrary to popular belief, colds are not caused by cold weather. Going outside on a wintry day will not make you any more likely to catch a cold. There are several different reasons that people usually get colds during the colder months. The main reason is that, in the winter, more people stay indoors and end up in close contact with one another.

The virus is usually transmitted by way of people's hands. That transfer doesn't only happen when people shake hands. It can also happen through objects that are touched by several people. For instance, if someone coughs on his or her hand and then touches a doorknob, the next person to touch the doorknob may pick up a virus. This transfer is practically unavoidable, so the best thing to do is simply to wash your hands. Also, you can try not to touch your nose or eyes, because they're easy landing zones for cold viruses, which take up residence in the cells inside the nose.

Although there are ways to reduce your exposure to colds, some scientists believe Americans suffer through as many as a billion colds per year. There's no relief in sight. For now, the common cold remains an unbeatable bug.

 Questions

1. What does the phrase "contrary to popular belief" mean in the ninth paragraph of this passage?

    A   ignoring what most people believe
    B   insulting what most people believe
    C   according to what most people believe
    D   different from what most people believe

 Tip

> If you're not sure what this phrase means, try to figure it out by looking at how it is
> used in the sentence. What do most people believe about colds and cold weather?
> Is their belief right or wrong?

2. Read the sentence below.

    The most annoying symptoms are actually caused by your own immune system, which does every-
    thing it can to eradicate the virus.

    What does the word <u>eradicate</u> mean in this sentence?

    A   get rid of
    B   surround
    C   create with
    D   absorb

 Tip

> If you don't know what this word means, read the sentence carefully. Think about
> what the article said about the immune system's role in dealing with viruses. What
> does your immune system want to do with the virus?

3. Read this sentence from the article.

Napoleon had a recipe for cold pills that he claimed worked wonders for him.

What does the author mean by the phrase "worked wonders"?

A   tasted great
B   worked well
C   was magical
D   worked sometimes

 Tip

Think about what the article says about Napoleon's cold pills. How did he feel about them? What did they do for him?

4. As used in this passage, what does the word <u>surefire</u> mean?

A   good
B   quick
C   certain
D   common

 Tip

When the author refers to "a surefire remedy," he or she means a cure.

Check your answers on the next page.

Passage 3: "The Common Cold: Unbeatable Bug?"

 Answers

1. D   Most people think that you can catch a cold by going outside in cold weather. The author is saying that this isn't true. Therefore, the phrase "contrary to what most people believe" means "different from what most people believe." Answer choice D is correct.

2. A   The word <u>eradicate</u>, as used in the sample sentence, means "to get rid of something." The immune system does not want to surround, create, or absorb the virus. It wants to eradicate it—get rid of it—completely.

3. B   You may have heard the term "worked wonders" before. It's a figurative phrase that means "proved very effective." Napoleon thought he had a great recipe for effective cold pills, which is probably why that recipe has been remembered over the centuries. Answer choice B is correct.

4. C   A surefire remedy for the common cold would be a certain cure. Answer choice C is the best answer.

Passage 4

Read this passage and answer the questions that follow.

The Invisible Tree

Wilfred Kramer was known all around town as a great illusionist. He was able to perform astounding card tricks and other clever tricks, and he always knew how to play a crowd. He would advertise himself aggressively, calling out to passersby and challenging them to try to outwit him and expose his secrets—and they never could.

Kramer sought to strengthen the public's perception of him as a world-class illusionist by doing more and more ambitious tricks. One evening he bragged that he could make the tallest tree in town disappear in the blink of an eye. Of course, the people who overheard his claim scoffed at the outrageous concept. The towering oak tree in front of the courthouse was over a hundred years old and it seemed to reach into the clouds. Obviously, making an object so huge disappear was <u>inconceivable</u>.

However, the people were secretly fascinated by Kramer's claim. They knew he would not risk damaging his reputation unless he actually knew of some spell that might make the tree disappear. The people hoped to catch a glimpse of any activities he was doing in preparation for his great trick. They weren't disappointed. Kramer had gathered large stacks of lumber, and he spent several days hammering them together in his yard.

"What's he making?" the people asked one another. Some speculated he was building a huge curtain to cover the tree—but there wasn't enough lumber for that.

Finally, Kramer answered their questions. "I've simply built a stage where people can sit to watch my greatest illusion ever," he proclaimed, showing off a sturdy seating platform. The people were satisfied with his explanation, but they were back to not knowing what sort of trick he had in mind.

The day after completing his stage, Kramer brought a large winch mechanism to his house. Some people saw him transporting the heavy machine, and they began to wonder what he'd do with it. Winches, they knew, were used to pull heavy weights—but no winch in the world was big enough to move the oak tree. But after a day, the winch had disappeared; all that remained in Kramer's yard was the stage.

A few days later, the illusionist rented a truck and transported the wooden stage to the courthouse lawn. Then he attached a wall to the front of the stage; in the center of the wall was an opening through which anyone on the stage could clearly see the oak tree. Dozens of people gathered on the lawn to marvel at the handcrafted stage and speculate on Kramer's next move.

However, there was no next move. Kramer simply announced that his greatest trick was scheduled for that very next evening, just after sundown. When that time approached, hundreds of people lined up to reserve a seat on the stage. When they sat down, they could see plainly through the opening in the stage wall that the oak tree was still there. Kramer had not done anything to it. He was not trying to conceal it with curtains, or lug it away using winches.

When the stage was filled, Kramer appeared in front of the crowd and waved to his audience. Then he tossed a small black cloth over the opening in the wall and began to recite what sounded like magical verses. The audience sat for several minutes in anxious silence, waiting to see the result of the illusionist's greatest trick ever. Then Kramer grabbed the black cloth and pulled it down. Nobody could see the tree through the opening.

"He made the tree disappear!" the audience shouted.

Kramer never <u>divulged</u> the secret of his disappearing trick—well, at least not to any person. He did tell his cat, though. He explained to his cat that he'd attached the winch to the bottom of the stage. After Kramer covered up the opening in the wall, he activated the winch. Ever so slowly, the winch had pulled the stage a few inches to the left. When Kramer pulled down the cloth, the tree was still there, just not in the audience's view. It appeared to them that, at least temporarily, Wilfred Kramer had made the tallest tree in town invisible!

 Questions

1.   What does the phrase "play a crowd" mean as it is used in the first paragraph of this passage?

     A   perform music for
     B   converse with
     C   recall stories
     D   interest people

 Tip

Look at the sentence that contains this phrase, and think about what the story tells you about Kramer. What was his special ability when it came to dealing with crowds? If you don't remember, look back to the story for hints.

2. As it is used in this passage, what does <u>inconceivable</u> mean?

    A   amazing
    B   exceptional
    C   unbelievable
    D   time-consuming

 Tip

    You can figure out the meaning to this word by looking at the context. Reread the sentence containing the word and then choose the best answer choice.

3. As used in this passage, what does the word <u>divulged</u> mean?

    A   told
    B   kept
    C   taught
    D   discovered

 Tip

    Reread the sentence containing the word. Did Kramer ever tell anyone his secret?

Check your answers on the next page.

Passage 4: "The Invisible Tree"

 Answers

1. D   The term "playing a crowd" refers to getting an audience interested and excited about what it is about to witness. Answer choice D is correct.

2. C   The people were shocked that Kramer said he could make such a huge tree disappear. Answer choice C is correct.

3. A   Kramer never told—or divulged—his secret to anyone. Answer choice A is the best answer.

Lesson 2: Inferences and Conclusions

Fiction

R8A.1.3 **Make inferences and draw conclusions based on text.**

- Make inferences and draw conclusions based on information from text.
- Cite evidence from text to support generalizations.

Nonfiction

R8A.2.3 **Make inferences and draw conclusions based on text.**

- Make inferences and draw conclusions based on information from text.
- Cite evidence from text to support generalizations.

R8B.3.1 **Differentiate from fact and opinion.**

- Identify a factual statement from text that supports an assertion, or identify an opinion.
- Analyze positions or arguments for evidence of statements of fact and opinion.

R8.B.3.2 **Distinguish between essential and nonessential information within or across texts.**

- Identify bias and propaganda where present.

R8.B.3.3 **Analyze text organization including sequence, question/answer, comparison/ contrast, cause and effect, problem/solution, the headings, graphics and charts to derive meaning.**

- Identify content that would fit in a specific section of text.
- Interpret graphics and charts, and make connections between text and the content of graphics and charts.

What are conclusions and inferences?

When you draw a **conclusion** or make an **inference**, you draw personal meaning from a passage. These types of questions are not stated in the passage, so you won't be able to put your finger on them. You have to determine the answer based on what you have read. In other words, you have to think carefully about what you have read.

When you draw a conclusion, you make a judgment or arrive at an opinion about something. When you make an inference, you often predict something that will happen based on the facts at hand. You might surmise or guess something about a person, idea, or thing. For example, suppose you are a reading a mystery novel. You are about halfway through it when you conclude that the maid did it, but you also infer that she is crafty and will try to frame the butler.

On the PSSA, questions asking you to draw a conclusion or make an inference often begin with "why" and/or include the words "probably" or "it is likely that." Questions might also ask you to identify a fact or an opinion. Remember that a fact can be proven and an opinion is what someone thinks.

Lastly, you might be asked how a passage is organized. For example, you might have to choose whether a passage is a comparison/contrast, a series of events in chronological order, or a different type of organization.

 **Activity**

Look at the picture above. Draw a conclusion about the two men. Make an inference about what they will do next. Share your conclusion and prediction with the class.

_____

_____

_____

_____

Passage 1

Now read this passage and then answer the questions that follow.

The Truth about Organ Donation

Myths about organ donation have circulated for decades, but most are simply stories invented by people who don't understand the process of organ donation. The truth is that the organs donated from one person's body can save multiple lives. The heart, kidneys, pancreas, lungs, and intestines all can be donated. In addition, eyes and body tissues, such as skin and bone marrow, can be donated. In the United States alone, over 87,000 people are on a waiting list to receive an organ, and these people may wait days, weeks, months, or even years, to receive an organ transplant. It is estimated that about ten to fourteen thousand people who die each year meet the requirements to be organ donors, but only about half of those people actually become organ donors. It is essential that you understand the facts about organ donation, so you can make the right choice when the time comes.

It might not be pleasant to think about what happens to a person's body after he or she passes away, but organ donors know that their organs will be used to save human lives. Many organ donors are victims of accidents or other unexpected traumas, and their organs are perfectly healthy when they arrive in the emergency room. Emergency room doctors work hard to save patients' lives, but sometimes the brain has been so severely damaged that it will never work again. If the brain shows no signs of activity and has no blood supply, doctors consider the brain dead, and the patient becomes a candidate for organ donation.

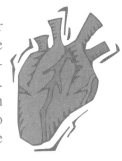

When a patient's family consents to donate the organs to someone in need, the patient is called a "donor." Doctors enter the organ donor's height, weight, and blood type into a computer, which searches for potential matches. The Organ Procurement and Transplantation Network maintains a list of people in need of organs. When a match is found, the patient who will receive the organ is prepared for the transplant surgery. A special team of physicians removes the necessary organs from the organ donor's body. Organs don't last very long outside the body, so once they have been removed they are quickly transported to the hospital where another surgical team is prepared to operate on the organ recipient. In some cases, the patient is ready to leave the hospital just a few days after the transplant surgery, but other times it takes longer for the patient to recover. Either way, most patients can eventually return to their normal lives,

INFERENCES AND CONCLUSIONS | Lesson 2

and live for many long, healthy years—all because a stranger was selfless enough to donate his or her organs to help save a life.

Becoming an organ donor is relatively easy; anyone, from a newborn baby to a great-great-grandmother, can become an organ donor. In many states, you can declare your organ donor status when you receive or renew your driver's license. You can also complete and carry an organ donor card in your wallet. If you choose to become an organ donor, you should talk to your family about your decision, and make them aware that if something happens to you, you want to donate your organs. Remember, when you make the decision to become an organ donor, you make the decision to save a life.

 Questions

1. Why do you think only half of the people eligible to donate organs actually donate them?

    _____

    _____

    _____

2. Why is it a good idea to inform your family if you decide to become an organ donor?

    _____

    _____

    _____

3. Do you think more people will donate organs in the future?

    _____

    _____

    _____

Check your answers on the next page.

Passage 1: "The Truth about Organ Donation"

 Answers

1. **Sample answer:** The reason that only half of those eligible to donate organs actually do so is that people do not like to think about their own death or giving their organs away. Many people are probably squeamish about this, and do not sign up to be organ donors. They may not realize the importance of the situation.

2. **Sample answer:** Your family might try to interfere if they do not realize that you would like your organs donated. Telling them of your intentions before the unthinkable happens will ensure that your organs go to someone in need.

3. **Sample answer:** I think more people will become organ donors in the future. As more and more people receive organ transplants and live longer than ever before, people will begin to realize that donating their organs is important and can save someone's life.

Passage 2

Now read this excerpt and then answer the questions that follow.

Excerpt from *Hard Times*
by Charles Dickens
CHAPTER I - THE ONE THING NEEDFUL

'NOW, what I want is, Facts. Teach these boys and girls nothing but Facts. Facts alone are wanted in life. Plant nothing else, and root out everything else. You can only form the minds of reasoning animals upon Facts: nothing else will ever be of any service to them. This is the principle on which I bring up my own children, and this is the principle on which I bring up these children. Stick to Facts, sir!'

The scene was a plain, bare, monotonous vault of a school-room, and the speaker's square fore-finger emphasized his observations by underscoring every sentence with a line on the schoolmaster's sleeve. The emphasis was helped by the speaker's square wall of a forehead, which had his eyebrows for its base, while his eyes found commodious cellarage in two dark caves, overshadowed by the wall. The emphasis was helped by the speaker's mouth, which was wide, thin, and hard set. The emphasis was helped by the speaker's voice, which was inflexible, dry, and dictatorial. The emphasis was helped by the speaker's hair, which bristled on the skirts of his bald head, a plantation of firs to keep the wind from its shining surface, all covered with knobs, like the crust of a plum pie, as if the head had scarcely warehouse-room for the hard facts stored inside. The speaker's obstinate carriage, square coat, square legs, square shoulders,—nay, his very neckcloth, trained to take him by the throat with an unaccom-modating grasp, like a stubborn fact, as it was,—all helped the emphasis.

'In this life, we want nothing but Facts, sir; nothing but Facts!'

The speaker, and the schoolmaster, and the third grown person present, all backed a little, and swept with their eyes the inclined plane of little vessels then and there arranged in order, ready to have imperial gallons of facts poured into them until they were full to the brim.

Questions

1. What can you conclude about the speaker's appearance?

   A He is very old.
   B He is not neat.
   C He is very strong.
   D He is not handsome.

Tip

Reread the description of the speaker's appearance. What image do you think the author is trying to create?

2. Why does the speaker keep repeating the word "facts"?

   A to stress his point
   B to scare the students
   C to clear up any confusion
   D to give the students information

Tip

Reread the first paragraph of the excerpt.

3. It is likely that the speaker is

   A the students' teacher
   B someone of high authority
   C a parent of one of the students
   D a friend of the schoolmaster

Tip

Reread the beginning and ending of the excerpt.

Check your answers on the next page.

INFERENCES AND CONCLUSIONS　　　　**Lesson 2**

Passage 2: Excerpt from "Hard Times"

 Answers

1. D   While answer choice C might also seem correct, we know that the speaker seems intimidating, but we really don't know if he is strong. The description of the speaker is definitely "not handsome." Answer choice D is the best answer.

2. A   Answer choice A is the best answer choice. The speaker is trying to stress the importance of the children learning "facts."

3. B   The speaker is not the students' teacher, since he tells someone to teach them facts in the beginning of the excerpt, so answer choice A is not the correct answer. He does not seem to be a parent, and we don't not know if he is a friend of the schoolmaster. Answer choice B is the best answer.

Passage 3

Now read this excerpt and then answer the questions that follow.

Space Colonization: Too Big a Risk

Just a few decades ago, the idea of establishing colonies in space was viewed as nothing more than a wild science-fiction tale. However, as technological advances and scientific discoveries teach us more about the places beyond our planet, space colonization looks increasingly possible. Within our lifetimes, we may see people making an effort to build a permanent city on another planet or even on an asteroid. Perhaps you or I will even travel to the stars for a vacation!

If you were able to vote today on whether or not another planet—the red planet Mars, for instance—should be colonized, would you vote "yes" or "no"? Many people are enthusiastic about this idea, and see it as an entirely positive opportunity for the people of Earth. These supporters of space colonization have many good ideas, but may be overlooking some other important information. Colonizing another planet would be one of the biggest steps ever taken in human history. An accomplishment that important carries along many dangers, expenses, and other concerns. Before you make your decision, you should be aware of the possible negative aspects of such an event.

First of all, the complications of establishing a livable city on another planet are staggering. Even the world's finest scientists are still baffled by the question of how they could keep people safe and healthy on the surface of an alien world. People require very special conditions in order to live, and it would be hard to ensure those conditions on an unexplored new world.

Of all the planets, Mars seems like it would best support human visitors—but it's still an inhospitable place. The atmosphere is so thin it would be impossible to breathe. People would need special equipment in order to get the air they need to live. It's possible that the first colonists would have to spend their entire lives wearing space suits. Also, temperatures on the red planet can become extremely cold—much colder than Antarctica. It might be possible for people to live in such temperatures, but few would find them comfortable!

Although there may have once been flowing water on Mars, today it is a very dry planet. Humans rely on water to live, and colonists would have to bring a large amount of it with them. Special machines would have to be developed in order to recycle the drinking water. Even if the water problem was solved, how would the colonists get food? The Martian ground is rocky and dry; it seems unlikely that any kind of Earth crops could possibly grow there. Until that was figured out, rockets would have to be constantly sent to the colony with fresh supplies; the cost of doing this would be huge.

INFERENCES AND CONCLUSIONS | Lesson 2

Additionally, the overall cost of a colonization mission would be downright breathtaking. Scientists have estimated the price tag of a single mission to be set at about $30 billion. That funding is desperately needed for projects here on our planet. Social programs of all sorts could benefit greatly from even a fraction of that amount. We humans would be wise to invest more time, money, and effort in improving our own world before we start visiting others.

That idea leads into one of the saddest but most important questions we must keep in mind during this age of amazing new technologies: can humans be trusted with a brand new planet? Humans have proven to be very imperfect guests, to say the least. The greatest threats to our current planet are posed by us, its inhabitants. Through weapons, warfare, pollution, and greed, humanity has taken advantage of the natural splendor that Earth once possessed. Some scientists believe that humans have a duty to spread out across the solar system and spread beauty and intelligence. However, over the centuries humans have spread just as much hatred and horror as they've spread beauty and intelligence.

Some supporters of space colonization believe that the nations of Earth would unify and work together to achieve this common goal. These supporters think that all aspects of Earth life, from education to economics, would be improved by the race to colonize space. However, a short survey of history points to opposite ideas.

History shows that colonization has caused greed, hatred, prejudice and war among the nations of Earth. Imagine the effects of space colonization! Nations would likely struggle to be first to reach the red planet; then they would struggle for the rights to build on the best land; then they would struggle for resources for their colonists. The results could be more mistrust, fear, and conflict. A Mars colony might end up further dividing the people of Earth and yielding more suffering than discovery.

Should a colonization project proceed despite these many problems, what sort of benefits would it bring to the people of Earth? Some scientists have suggested that we build mines in space, to gather valuable metals like iron and gold from asteroids and other celestial bodies. This would return some of the costs of the mission. However, our planet is already well equipped with dozens of types of metal and minerals. In fact, with Earth's natural resources as well as our recycling programs, we have more than enough already. Besides, if we were to build colonies just to make money, greedy competition would no doubt arise that would endanger the whole project.

Some scientists have proclaimed that colonizing the red planet would ensure the survival of the human race. Their argument is that, even if Earth were to die or be destroyed, a group of humans would still exist in their Martian colony. This argument may be true, but it's not a strong argument because it doesn't apply to our world's current situation. Earth is still a healthy and vital planet and promises to remain that way for a very long time. The human race is growing every year and is definitely not endangered. We humans can live on for millions of years longer on Earth, if only we learn to behave more responsibly.

In conclusion, the concept of space colonization is a fascinating one, but it is fraught with problems and dangers. There may be a time when humans are ready to build their cities on the surface of Mars. However, attempting to conquer Mars now, while neglecting Earth, might bring enormous damage to Earth and its inhabitants.

Lesson 2   **INFERENCES AND CONCLUSIONS**

Questions

1. What is probably the main reason some people would like to live in space?

    A   to escape from conflict
    B   to learn more about Earth
    C   to prove that it can be done
    D   to profit from the experience

 Tip

Reread the beginning of the passage. What do you think is the main reason some people would like to be part of a space colony?

2. What is the author's strongest reason against space colonization?

    A   fear
    B   cost
    C   danger
    D   conflict

 Tip

Reread the passage and choose the answer choice that seems to be his most important reason.

3. Why do you think the author believes that the human race will survive on Earth for many more years to come?

    A   The population is increasing.
    B   Technology is advancing quickly.
    C   Medical advances are being made.
    D   Conflict among nations has been reduced.

 Tip

Reread the end of the passage. Consider why the author thinks the future of the human race is not in danger on Earth.

INFERENCES AND CONCLUSIONS   Lesson 2

4. Do you think a space colony will be established during the next few decades? Why or why not?

_____

_____

_____

5. Find a sentence in the passage that states an opinion and write it here.

_____

_____

_____

6. Which **best** describes the organizational pattern of this passage?

   A   cause and effect
   B   in order of sequence
   C   compare and contrast
   D   in order of importance

Check your answers on the next page.

Lesson 2 | **INFERENCES AND CONCLUSIONS**

Passage 3: "Space Colonization: Too Big a Risk"

 Answers

1. C   The passage implies that people would like to live in space to prove it can be done. If you were unsure of this answer, you could have chosen it simply by process of elimination. The other answer choices are not implied in the passage.

2. B   While the author indicates that establishing a space colony is dangerous, the main reason he is against it is cost. Answer choice B is the best answer.

3. A   If you reread the end of the article, you can conclude that the author believes the human race will continue to exist on Earth because the population is increasing.

4.   **Sample answer:** While we might be able to establish a space colony, I don't think this will happen during our lifetime. As the author states, it simply costs too much money. We need to take care of everyone on our planet first. I think the American public would be strongly against spending this much money to establish a space colony.

5.   **Sample answers:** "Within our lifetimes, we may see people making an effort to build a permanent city on another planet or even on an asteroid."

"Additionally, the overall cost of a colonization mission would be downright breathtaking."

"Humans have proven to be very imperfect guests, to say the least."

. . . or other opinion in the passage.

6. D   Most of the text is organized in order of importance in a way that is as persuasive as possible. Answer choice D is the best answer.

Excerpt from *The Secret Garden*
by Frances Hodgson Burnett
from Chapter 15 – "Nest Building"

In her talks with Colin, Mary had tried to be very cautious about the secret garden. There were certain things she wanted to find out from him, but she felt that she must find them out without asking him direct questions. In the first place, as she began to like to be with him, she wanted to discover whether he was the kind of boy you could tell a secret to. He was not in the least like Dickon, but he was evidently so pleased with the idea of a garden no one knew anything about that she thought perhaps he could be trusted. But she had not known him long enough to be sure. The second thing she wanted to find out was this: If he could be trusted—if he really could—wouldn't it be possible to take him to the garden without having any one find it out? The grand doctor had said that he must have fresh air and Colin had said that he would not mind fresh air in a secret garden. Perhaps if he had a great deal of fresh air and knew Dickon and the robin and saw things growing he might not think so much about dying. Mary had seen herself in the glass sometimes lately when she had realized that she looked quite a different creature from the child she had seen when she arrived from India. This child looked nicer. Even Martha had seen a change in her.

On that first morning when the sky was blue again Mary wakened very early. The sun was pouring in slanting rays through the blinds and there was something so joyous in the sight of it that she jumped out of bed and ran to the window. She drew up the blinds and opened the window itself and a great waft of fresh, scented air blew in upon her. The moor was blue and the whole world looked as if something Magic had happened to it. There were tender little fluting sounds here and there and everywhere, as if scores of birds were beginning to tune up for a concert. Mary put her hand out of the window and held it in the sun.

"It's warm—warm!" she said. "It will make the green points push up and up and up, and it will make the bulbs and roots work and struggle with all their might under the earth."

She kneeled down and leaned out of the window as far as she could, breathing big breaths and sniffing the air until she laughed because she remembered what Dickon's mother had said about the end of his nose quivering like a rabbit's. "It must be very early," she said. "The little clouds are all pink and I've never seen the sky look like this. No one is up. I don't even hear the stable boys."

A sudden thought made her scramble to her feet.

"I can't wait! I am going to see the garden!" . . .

When she had reached the place where the door hid itself under the ivy, she was startled by a curious loud sound. It was the caw–caw of a crow and it came from the top of the wall, and when she looked up, there sat a big glossy-plumaged blue-black bird, looking down at her very wisely indeed. She had never seen a crow so close before and he made her a little nervous, but the next moment he spread his wings and flapped away across the garden. She hoped he was not going to stay inside and she pushed the door open wondering if he would. When she got fairly into the garden she saw that he probably did intend to stay because he had alighted on a dwarf apple-tree and under the apple-tree was lying a little reddish animal with a Bushy tail, and both of them were watching the stooping body and rust-red head of Dickon, who was kneeling on the grass working hard.

Mary flew across the grass to him.

"Oh, Dickon! Dickon!" she cried out. "How could you get here so early! How could you! The sun has only just got up!"

He got up himself, laughing and glowing, and tousled; his eyes like a bit of the sky.

"Eh!" he said. "I was up long before him. How could I have stayed abed! Th' world's all fair begun again this mornin', it has. An' it's workin' an' hummin' an' scratchin' an' pipin' an' nest-buildin' an' breathin' out scents, till you've got to be out on it 'stead o' lyin' on your back. When th' sun did jump up, th' moor went mad for joy, an' I was in the midst of th' heather, an' I run like mad myself, shoutin' an' singin'. An' I come straight here. I couldn't have stayed away. Why, th' garden was lyin' here waitin'!"

Mary put her hands on her chest, panting, as if she had been running herself.

"Oh, Dickon! Dickon!" she said. "I'm so happy I can scarcely breathe!"

Seeing him talking to a stranger, the little bushy-tailed animal rose from its place under the tree and came to him, and the rook, cawing once, flew down from its branch and settled quietly on his shoulder.

"This is th' little fox cub," he said, rubbing the little reddish animal's head. "It's named Captain. An' this here's Soot. Soot he flew across th' moor with me an' Captain he run same as if th' hounds had been after him. They both felt same as I did."

Neither of the creatures looked as if he were the least afraid of Mary. When Dickon began to walk about, Soot stayed on his shoulder and Captain trotted quietly close to his side.

"See here!" said Dickon. "See how these has pushed up, an' these an' these! An' Eh! Look at these here!"

He threw himself upon his knees and Mary went down beside him. They had come upon a whole clump of crocuses burst into purple and orange and gold. Mary bent her face down and kissed and kissed them. . . . There was every joy on earth in the secret garden that morning, and in the midst of them came a delight more delightful than all, because it was more wonderful. Swiftly something flew across the wall and darted through the trees to a close grown corner, a little flare of red-breasted bird with something hanging from its beak. Dickon stood quite still and put his hand on Mary almost as if they had suddenly found themselves laughing in a church.

INFERENCES AND CONCLUSIONS   **Lesson 2**

"We munnot stir," he whispered in broad Yorkshire. "We munnot scarce breathe. I knowed he was mate-huntin' when I seed him last. It's Ben Weatherstaff's robin. He's buildin' his nest. He'll stay here if us don't fight him." They settled down softly upon the grass and sat there without moving . . . .

Mistress Mary was not at all sure that she knew, as Dickon seemed to, how to try to look like grass and trees and bushes. But he had said the queer thing as if it were the simplest and most natural thing in the world, and she felt it must be quite easy to him, and indeed she watched him for a few minutes carefully, wondering if it was possible for him to quietly turn green and put out branches and leaves. But he only sat wonderfully still, and when he spoke dropped his voice to such a softness that it was curious that she could hear him, but she could.

"It's part o' th' springtime, this nest-buildin' is," he said. "I warrant it's been goin' on in th' same way every year since th' world was begun. They've got their way o' thinkin' and doin' things an' a body had better not meddle. You can lose a friend in springtime easier than any other season if you're too curious." . . .

He made one of his low whistling calls and the robin turned his head and looked at him inquiringly, still holding his twig. Dickon spoke to him as Ben Weatherstaff did, but Dickon's tone was one of friendly advice . . . .

"Tha' knows us won't trouble thee," he said to the robin. "Us is near bein' wild things ourselves. Us is nest-buildin' too, bless thee. Look out tha' doesn't tell on us."

And though the robin did not answer, because his beak was occupied, Mary knew that when he flew away with his twig to his own corner of the garden the darkness of his dew-bright eye meant that he would not tell their secret for the world.

 # Questions

1. Why does Mary look different from when she first arrived from India?

   A   She is happier.
   B   She is smarter.
   C   She is healthier.
   D   She has grown up.

 # Tip

Think about the way Mary acts. Which conclusion is most likely?

Lesson 2 | **INFERENCES AND CONCLUSIONS**

2. Why doesn't Mary ask Colin the things she would like to know about him?

    A   She doesn't want to be rude.

    B   She doesn't know if he'll be honest.

    C   She isn't sure if fresh air will be good for him.

    D   She isn't sure if Dickon will be upset with her.

Tip
Carefully reread the beginning of the excerpt.

3. What can you conclude about Dickon?

_____

_____

_____

_____

_____

_____

Tip
What does Dickon do that is unusual?

Check your answers on the next page.

Passage 4: Excerpt from "The Secret Garden"

 Answers

1. A   Mary is much happier now. She is thrilled that it is spring and she values her friendship with Dickon. The narrator says that Mary looks nicer and remarks later in the excerpt that she notices things she would not have six months ago.

2. A   The beginning of the excerpt says that Mary feels she must find things out about Colin without asking him directly. This leads you to conclude that she doesn't want to offend him. Answer choice A is the best answer.

3.   **Sample answer:** Dickon loves nature and has a unique way with animals that is likely unrealistic. He plays with and talks to a fox cub and a crow lands on his shoulder. He names these animals and considers them his friends.

Lesson 3: Main Idea

Fiction

R8.A.1.4   **Identify and explain main ideas and relevant details.**

- Identify and/or explain stated or implied main ideas and relevant supporting details from text.

R8.A.1.5   **Summarize a fictional text as a whole.**

- Summarize the key details and events of a fictional text as a whole.

Nonfiction

R8.A.2.4   **Identify and explain main ideas and relevant details.**

- Identify and/or explain stated or implied main ideas and relevant supporting details from text.

R8.A.2.5   **Summarize a nonfictional text as a whole.**

- Summarize the major points, processes, and/or events of a nonfictional text as a whole.

What is the main idea?

The **main idea** is the essential message of a passage. Sometimes the main idea is stated in a passage, meaning you can actually put your finger on a sentence or two expressing the main idea. Other times the main idea is not stated and you have to determine it from the information in the passage.

Supporting details explain and expand upon the main idea. They provide more information about the main idea. Supporting details might be facts, examples, or description.

PSSA test questions about the main idea might ask you what the passage is mostly about or to choose the best summary of a passage. They might also ask you to identify the main idea of a paragraph in the passage. They may even ask you to identify or correctly interpret important supporting details.

 **Activity 1**

Read the following paragraph. Think about the main idea, what the whole paragraph is about, as you read. Then fill in the graphic organizer underneath the paragraph.

Ancient Egyptian physicians were very advanced for their time, but some of their "cures" for illnesses and diseases were way off base. While these physicians had some clinical knowledge, meaning they based some of their treatment on science, they were also very superstitious and offered their patients magical cures. If you lived in ancient Egypt and had a stomach ache, your doctor might tell you to crush a hog's tooth and put it inside of a sugar cake and eat it. To cure a headache, your doctor would advise you to fry a catfish skull in oil and rub this oil on your head. If you had trouble with your eyes, your physician would mix together special ingredients, including parts of a pig, put the mixture in your ear, and say, "I have brought this thing and put it in its place. The crocodile is weak and powerless."

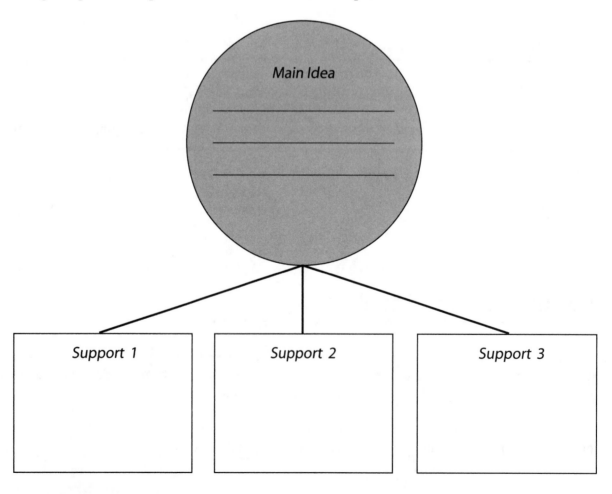

Activity 2

Break into groups of about four or five. Write a paragraph using one of the following sentences as the main idea.

- My summer vacation was really great last year.

- Sometimes you can learn an important lesson from making a big mistake.

- Heroes come in all shapes and sizes.

Passage 1

Now read this passage. Think about the main idea as you read. Then answer the questions that follow.

The Trail of Tears

The United States signed the Declaration of Independence in 1776. Soon after, the nation began to grow by leaps and bounds. Both population and territories increased. As European settlers explored new lands and pushed further into the frontier, they forced many Native Americans out of their homelands. By 1830, settlers had flooded into Georgia and increased the population of the state several times over. The Cherokee Indians were also living in Georgia at the time and had lived there for many years.

For a while, the settlers and the Cherokee shared the land and resided together peacefully. The Cherokee adapted to the European way of life that the settlers brought with them to America. The discovery of gold on Cherokee lands, however, prompted the settlers to urge the United States government to remove the Cherokee from their homeland. The removal of Native American peoples from their home territories created more space for settlers and allowed them to take control of the valuable resources found on the land. Such "removal" was quite common during this time as many other Native Americans had been forced to move west of the Mississippi River. While the removal was good for the settlers, it was devastating for the Native Americans.

In 1835, a small group of Cherokee leaders signed the Treaty of Enchota. Even though most of the Cherokee disagreed with the treaty, it allowed President Andrew Jackson to order the removal of the Cherokee from their lands in Georgia to areas west of the Mississippi. In 1838, General Winfield Scott and seven thousand men began removing the Cherokee from their homeland. The troops gathered Cherokee men, women, and children in shabby camps with little shelter and food. Then, they forced the Cherokee to march one thousand miles from Georgia to Oklahoma during the fall and winter of 1838.

Many of the Cherokee fell ill or died along the way. Troops did not allow time to stop and grieve for lost loved ones, causing the Cherokee to label their march *"Nunna dual Tsuny,"* or "The Trail of Tears." By the time the Cherokee reached Oklahoma, they had lost more than four thousand of their friends, relatives, and loved ones. It was one of the saddest events in the United States' brief history.

Questions

1. Write a phrase telling what this passage is mostly about.

    _____

2. Now, write a sentence expressing the main idea of this passage.

    _____

    _____

3. Identify three supporting details in the passage.

    _____

    _____

    _____

    Check your answers on the next page.

Passage 1: "The Trail of Tears"

 Answers

1. Your answer should contain a phrase, such as "trail of tears," or "Native Americans forced to move."

2. Your answer should contain a sentence stating what the passage is about, such as "The passage is mostly about the Cherokee being forced to move to Oklahoma and the pain they suffered during this move."

3. Remember that supporting details expand upon the main idea. Here are some supporting details, but there are others!

   a. The settlers urged the Unites States government to remove the Cherokee from their homeland when they discovered gold on the land.

   b. The removal was good for the settlers, but it was terrible for the Cherokee.

   c. When the Cherokee reached Oklahoma, they had lost more than four thousand of their loved ones.

Passage 2

Read this passage. Think about its main idea as you read. When you finish reading the passage, answer the questions that follow.

The Birth of Golf
by Nathan Barrett

In the 1400s, farmers in eastern Scotland invented a simple but ingenious new pastime. It was a sport that required only simple, easily improvised equipment: sticks and round pebbles. This sport was perfectly suited to the geography of the Scottish coast, which included grassy tracks, sand dunes, and rabbit holes. The makeshift entertainment would evolve over generations into the game we know today as golf.

This early form of golf had an immediate impact on the people of Scotland. It was immensely popular among the citizens, who were so enthusiastic about the game that they devoted much of their time to it. They spent so much time playing golf, in fact, that they neglected their duty to King James II by shrugging off their obligation to train for the military. The enraged king, seeing that his military might suffer because his people were spending all their time playing with sticks and pebbles, declared golf illegal in 1457.

The outlook for the new sport brightened again almost fifty years later, when King James IV discovered that the banned pastime was actually quite entertaining. Not only did he lift the ban, but his interest in the sport—like a celebrity endorsement today—made golf more popular than ever. The royalty of England and Scotland began teaching foreign rulers how to golf.

The sport took hold in France, but the heart of golf remained in Scotland. The capital of the country, Edinburgh, hosted the world's most famous golf course, which was called Leith. In 1744, the first golfers' organization, the Gentleman Golfers, formed at Leith. They originated the idea of golf tournaments, yearly competitions featuring impressive trophy prizes. Additionally, they devised a set of rules for the game that were widely accepted.

Golf had come a long way since the sticks and stones used in the 1400s. By the 1700s, specially designed clubs and balls were being handcrafted by exclusive shops. Club handles were made mostly from special kinds of wood. Many early clubs also had heads made of wood, though some heads were made of blacksmith-forged iron. Today, most clubs are made entirely of lightweight, super-strong metal. Even with these improvements, golf in the modern era is essentially the same game Scottish farmers played six hundred years ago.

 Questions

1. The first golf game required only sticks and

    A   iron
    B   balls
    C   rocks
    D   pebbles

 Tip

This question asks about a supporting detail. Go back and reread the beginning of the passage.

2. The second paragraph of this passage is mainly about

    A   how King James II felt about golf
    B   how people in Scotland felt about golf
    C   what people in Scotland used to play golf
    D   how people in Scotland played the game of golf

 Tip

Reread the paragraph. Choose the answer choice that tells what the entire paragraph is about.

3. This passage is mainly about

   A how golf began in Scotland
   B how the game of golf got started
   C the history of golf throughout the world
   D the way people feel about playing golf

 Tip

The title of the article will give you a clue to the answer of this question.

Now check your answers on the next page. Read the explanations after each answer.

Passage 2: "The Birth of Golf"

 Answers

1. C   The beginning of the passage says that people first played golf with sticks and pebbles.

2. B   The main idea of paragraph two is how people in Scotland felt about golf. The other answer choices are supporting details.

3. B   The entire passage is about how the game of golf got started. While answer choice C might also seem correct, the passage does not present the entire history of golf, just its beginnings.

Passage 3

Read the following poem and answer the questions that follow.

The Lamplighter
by Robert Louis Stevenson

My tea is nearly ready and the sun has left the sky.
It's time to take the window to see Leerie going by;
For every night at teatime and before you take your seat,
With lantern and with ladder he comes posting up the street.

Now Tom would be a driver and Maria go to sea,
And my papa's a banker and as rich as he can be;
But I, when I am stronger and can choose what I'm to do,
O Leerie, I'll go round at night and light the lamps with you!

For we are very lucky, with a lamp before the door,
And Leerie stops to light it as he lights so many more;
And oh! before you hurry by with ladder and with light;
O Leerie, see a little child and nod to him to-night!

 Questions

1. This poem is mainly about a

   A   lamplighter named Leerie
   B   child who wants to see a lamplighter
   C   child who likes to look out the window each night
   D   child who wonders what to be when he grows up

 Tip

Choose the answer choice that tells what the entire poem is about. Consider who is speaking in the poem.

2. When does Leerie light the lamps?

   A   in the evening
   B   in the morning
   C   in the afternoon
   D   during the night

Tip

This question asks about a supporting detail. Reread the first line of the poem.

3. Write a summary of the poem. Use at least three details from the poem.

_____

_____

_____

Tip

Figure out the meaning of each stanza of the poem. Then write your essay.

Check your answers on the next page.

Passage 3: "The Lamplighter"

 Answers

1. B   While the first answer choice might also seem correct, the child is an important part of the poem along with the lamplighter. Answer choice B includes both the child and the lamplighter, so it is the best answer choice.

2. A   The beginning of the poem says that Leerie lights the lamps when the sun sets, so answer choice A is the best answer.

3.   **Sample answer:** The poem is about a child who might be sick who sits by the window each evening to watch Leerie, the lamplighter use a lantern and a ladder to light the lamps. The child says that when he is stronger, he wants to be a lamplighter like Leerie and hopes that Leerie will see him and nod.

Passage 4

Read this passage. Think about its main idea as you read. When you finish reading the passage, answer the questions that follow.

Mosquitoes: Annoying but Amazing

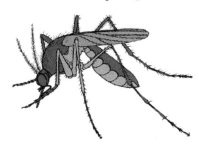

While the warm, sunny weather in Florida makes outdoor activities, such as picnics, swimming, parades, and sporting events enjoyable, pesky mosquitoes may be lurking nearby eager to interfere with your fun. Mosquitoes are tiny little creatures that bite people, make them itch, and sometimes even transmit diseases. While mosquitoes are annoying and sometimes hazardous, they are also interesting little pests.

Of all the insects, the mosquito is most similar to the fly. They both have wings, compound eyes, and three main body segments: a head, a thorax, and an abdomen. Basically, the mosquito is a skinny fly with longer legs and a tube (called a *proboscis* [pra-BAH-sis]) for a mouth. In fact, the word "mosquito" is Spanish for "little fly."

Don't let the name fool you, though. These "little flies" are highly advanced and specialized creatures. More than two thousand types of mosquitoes live in the world and they've been around for over thirty million years—far longer than humans. Over the millennia, mosquitoes have developed a wide range of abilities, which help them survive and make them difficult to outsmart.

Mosquitoes' greatest abilities are their acute senses, which they use to find food. Their main sensors specialize in detecting three things: chemicals, visual cues (color and motion), and heat.

Mosquitoes can smell the chemicals that people and animals give off when they breathe and sweat. Mosquitoes can find these chemicals in the air from as far as one hundred feet away! As they close in on their target, mosquitoes use their compound eyes to see motion and color. Then, at the closest range, they can sense the body heat of their intended victim. They can tell just where to go to find the best meal. Their three main sensors make them great hunters.

Once they find a source of food, they have a strange and famous way of eating—bloodsucking. They poke their tiny, sharp proboscises into people and animals and take tiny sips of blood. Don't worry about losing your blood, though. The amount a mosquito can drink is so small that you won't even notice it's gone.

The most annoying thing about mosquito bites is that they itch. This itching is caused by anticoagulants, chemicals that the mosquito uses to prevent your blood from clotting. (The bug knows that if your blood dries quickly near the bite, it won't be able to drink any more.) Your body reacts to the anticoagulants by swelling the area around the bite. The result is an itchy bump called a *wheal*. While the wheal is there, your immune system is busy cleaning away the anticoagulants.

Although people have an instinct to scratch mosquito bites, your doctor will tell you that this is not the best idea. Scratching can damage the skin or cause the bite to become infected. The best thing to do is to just wash a mosquito bite with soap and water and apply anti-itch medicine.

Mosquito bites are seldom dangerous but it is best to avoid being bitten whenever possible. Mosquitoes have been known to carry diseases that are harmful to humans and some people are allergic to mosquitoes and may become ill if bitten.

These persistent little pests are hard to beat, but there are several precautions which can help you avoid them. Since mosquitoes are most active during the morning and evening, you might try staying inside during those times of day. Put screens in your windows to keep them out of your house. If you do go out, wear extra clothing that covers your skin. This will make it harder for mosquitoes to bother you. Use mosquito repellents to confuse the insects' senses and make them pass you by.

You can also reduce the mosquito population. Mosquitoes lay their eggs in standing water, which is water that doesn't move or evaporate. Standing water might accumulate in buckets, barrels, and neglected swimming pools. You can help keep mosquitoes out of your neighborhood by getting rid of standing water.

Some scientists want to go even further to fight mosquitoes. At the Veterinary Entomology's Mosquito and Fly Research Unit in Gainesville, Florida, scientists have found a new weapon called a *baculovirus* (bah-cu-LOE-VĬR-us), a kind of tiny parasite found in dead mosquitoes in Florida. The scientists hope that this parasite could be used to kill the most harmful types of mosquitoes. Someday this amazing, annoying, airborne pest may be controlled.

 Questions

1. What is the primary topic of the second paragraph?

    A   A mosquito is a lot like a fly.
    B   The word mosquito means "little fly."
    C   A mosquito has a long tube for a mouth.
    D   Mosquitoes have three main body segments.

 Tip

Two answer choices identify supporting details in the paragraph. The other tells a fact that is not the main idea of the paragraph. The opening sentence of the paragraph provides a clue to the correct answer.

2. According to the article, what is the main reason you should avoid scratching mosquito bites?

    A   You will cause a wheal.
    B   You might harm your skin.
    C   You will make it itch more.
    D   You might cause it to spread.

 Tip

Reread paragraphs 7 and 8. Look for the reason you should not scratch mosquito bites.

3. How do mosquitoes find food? Use details and information from the article in your answer.

_____

_____

_____

 Tip

This is a short-response question. You have to write out the answer to this question. Find the section in the article that explains how mosquitoes find food. Reread this information. Then write your answer in your own words.

MAIN IDEA | **Lesson 3**

4. According to the article, what are the author's ideas about preventing mosquito bites?

_____

_____

_____

_____

_____

Tip

This is an extended-response question. Your answer for this type of question should be longer than an answer for a short-response question. Reread paragraphs 9, 10, and 11. Then write in your own words how you can prevent mosquito bites. When you finish, review the section "Beat the Bug" to be sure that you have mentioned each of the author's ideas.

Check your answers on the next page.

Passage 4: "Mosquitoes: Annoying but Amazing"

 Answers

1. A   The second paragraph explains how a mosquito is like a fly. This is what the paragraph is mostly about. The other answer choices present supporting details in this paragraph.

2. B   The article says that you should avoid scratching mosquito bites because you might damage your skin. Therefore, answer choice B is correct.

3.   **Sample answer:** Mosquitoes find food by using their incredible senses. They can smell the chemicals that people and animals give off when they sweat. They can do this from a hundred feet away. Once they get close to their target, they find it by using their eyes to see motion and color. When they are very close, they sense the body heat of the person or animal.

4.   **Sample answer:** The author recommends preventing mosquito bites whenever possible. He or she says that it is very hard to prevent mosquito bites, but you should try staying indoors in the morning and evening, the times of day when mosquitoes are most active. When you do go out, wear extra clothing that covers your skin. You should also use mosquito repellent to confuse their senses. The author also recommends getting rid of standing water, water that does not move or evaporate, since this is where mosquitoes lay their eggs.

Lesson 4: Author's Purpose

Fiction

R8.A.1.6 **Identify, describe, and analyze genre of text.**

- Identify and/or analyze the author's intended purpose of text.

- Explain, describe, and/or analyze examples of text that support the author's intended purpose.

Nonfiction

R8.A.2.6 **Identify, describe, and analyze genre of text.**

- Identify and/or describe the author's intended purpose of text.

- Explain, describe, and/or analyze examples of text that support the author's intended purpose.

Authors create pieces of writings for many reasons. They might write a short story to entertain readers or to teach a lesson. They might write an article that gives readers information or teaches them how to do something. Authors sometimes write articles or letter to convince readers to feel as they do or to persuade readers to take a certain action.

Questions about an author's purpose might ask you to identify the purpose of a piece of writing. You might have to decide if a passage is meant to entertain, inform, persuade, or instruct. You might also be asked to identify a statement that the author would agree with based on a passage you have read.

Activity 1

Determine the author's purpose for each sentence or group of sentences below. Write entertain, inform, teach, or persuade in the left-hand column.

Author's Purpose	Sentence
1.	It rained three inches yesterday.
2.	Everyone should recycle unwanted paper.
3.	Once upon a time, there lived a happy little rabbit named Bounce.
4.	Before you begin cleaning your room, you should get rid of all unnecessary clutter.
5.	The author George Eliot was actually a woman writing under a pen name.

Activity 2

In groups of 4 or 5 students, write a convincing advertisement for "Pearly White Toothpaste." Be sure to use persuasive words.

_____

_____

_____

_____

_____

_____

Passage 1

Think about the author's purpose as you read the following passage. Then answer the questions that follow.

How to Set up an Aquarium

Over the last century, fish have consistently been one of America's most preferred pets. Compared to most popular domestic animals, fish are low-maintenance creatures. They're well-behaved, too. It's hard to imagine a fish gnawing on furniture, shredding curtains, or shedding fur!

Setting up an aquarium can be an enjoyable project that calls on you to not only choose the conditions that would most benefit the fish, but also to make creative decisions that make the aquarium a piece of aquatic art. In order to construct an aquarium that's safe for fish and pleasing to the eye, follow these general guidelines. For more specific information, consult a specialist at your local pet shop.

What You'll Need
- Aquarium (glass or plastic)
- Water
- Filter
- Water Heater
- Water Pump
- Gravel
- Fish
- Fish Food

NOTE: Aquariums come in a wide variety of shapes and sizes, from the traditional goldfish bowl to massive tanks equal in size to some rooms. In selecting an appropriately sized aquarium, consider how many fish you intend to keep in it. To allow your fish to live comfortably, you should generally provide at least one gallon of water per fish.

Once you've acquired the necessary materials, the first step is to cleanse the aquarium of any grime, sediments, or other refuse that may have accumulated in it. Avoid using cleaning chemicals, though, since they can contaminate the water you later add to the aquarium. Once the aquarium is clean, add gravel to the bottom, typically one pound per gallon of water. You can even accessorize your aquarium with rocks or plants.

You'll want to install a filter in order to remove contaminants from the water and keep your fish healthy. Select a filter that's suitable for the size of your aquarium, and then install it according to the directions.

The next step is to fill the aquarium with clean, cool water; a safe guideline here is to only utilize water that you would consider drinkable. Don't fill the aquarium right to the top, though, because there are still a few subsequent items you'll need to add, including the water heater and pump. Install these appliances according to their directions. Usually, the heater should be adjusted to keep the water at a temperature of about seventy-five degrees Fahrenheit.

Then the fish will be more comfortable and healthy—unless you forget to add them! The most crucial component of an aquarium is, of course, the fish. Add them to the water and enjoy your new flippered friends.

 Questions

1. Why did the author write this passage?

   _____

   _____

2. Why did the author include the "Note" in this passage?

   _____

   _____

3. How do you think the author of this passage feels about fish?

   _____

   _____

Check your answers on the next page.

Passage 1: "How to Set up an Aquarium"

 Answers

1. Your answer should state that the author wrote this passage to teach readers how to set up an aquarium.

2. **Sample answer:** The author included the "Note" to explain that you should match the size of the fish tank you buy to the type of fish you plan to keep in it.

3. Your answer should explain that the author of the passage likes fish. The author takes care to give advice to ensure that fish in a tank are comfortable and healthy.

Passage 2

Think about the author's purpose as you read this passage. Then answer the questions that follow.

The Frame

When Vincent was young, he was accustomed to visiting his grandfather every weekend. They would spend many idle hours puttering in the workshop, with Pop devising and engineering new pieces of furniture and Vincent assisting him.

When Pop wouldn't need help for a while, Vince would go to his own corner of the small workshop, where he would practice with various tools and even attempt to invent his own creations—though he never became overly proficient at it. The best he could ever construct was a crude coat rack, using a scrap of wood and five bent nails. He usually wouldn't pay enough attention to his work because he'd be lost in conversation with Pop.

One weekend when Vince was eleven, his mother informed him that he couldn't visit Pop because he wasn't feeling well enough to entertain company. Vince, imagining it was a minor ailment, like a cold or a headache, didn't think much of it at the time. When the same thing occurred the next weekend, however, he became concerned. Soon realization dawned on Vince that his grandfather was seriously ill. Around a year later, after several months of declining health, Pop passed away.

Vince was devastated when he received the distressing news. He couldn't even fathom the loss of his grandfather—he couldn't conceive of never spending another weekend with Pop. Afterwards, he didn't even want to approach Pop's house, never mind the workshop.

When Vince was fourteen, he was informed that Pop's house would be auctioned and that this would be his last opportunity to say goodbye to the workshop. At first he told his mother that he didn't want to go because he thought it would be dispiriting. Afterwards, though, Vince looked around his own home at all the fine handcrafted furniture Pop had supplied: several chairs, a bookcase, a shadow box, three shelves, and other things. And then he knew what he should do.

Vince revisited the old workshop, and he discovered that it was not as depressing as he'd feared. This was because it reminded him of so many cheerful weekends—and, in fact, it sort of felt like Pop was still there. Vincent headed to his corner of the shop and gathered the tools he had used to construct the shoddy coat rack years ago. He toiled with lumber, saws, hammers, and nails for hours, all the while recalling the lessons Pop had taught him.

At the end of the day he brought home the finished product. It was a picture frame, made with the same skill and care that Pop had employed. Putting a picture of his grandfather in the frame, Vince hung it on the wall and smiled, thinking, *Pop would have been proud.*

 # Questions

1. The author would likely agree with which statement?

   A   People should put the past behind them.
   B   It is good to remember those we have lost.
   C   Woodworking is a very difficult skill to learn.
   D   Vince should spend time with those his own age.

 # Tip

Go back and reread the story. What point is the author trying to make?

2. The author wants us to think that Vince is

   A   afraid of the past.
   B   shy and sensitive.
   C   unsure of his future.
   D   caring and attentive.

 # Tip

How does Vince feel about Pop? What does this tell you about his character?

3. The main purpose of this passage is to

    A   narrate
    B   inform
    C   describe
    D   instruct

Tip

What kind of passage is this? Is a poem? A short story? An article?

4. What kind of person does the author want readers to think that Pop was? Use two examples from the story to support your answer.

    _____

    _____

    _____

Tip

Reread the beginning of the story. Why does Vince enjoy spending time with Pop?

Check your answers on the next page.

Passage 2: "The Frame"

 Answers

1. B   When Vince visits Pop's house, it is not as depressing as he thinks it will be. He enjoys remembering the time he spent with Pop. Answer choice B is the correct answer.

2. D   Vince is caring and attentive. He cares for Pop and has learned some valuable skills from spending time with him.

3. A   The main purpose of this passage is to tell a story or narrate. Answer choice A is the best answer.

4.   **Sample answer:** Pop was a very loving grandfather. His grandson, Vince, was often lost in conversation with him while working, so Pop must have been enjoyed spending time with Vince and talking to him. When Pop passes away, Vince can't imagine not spending another weekend with him, obviously because he had a special relationship with Pop.

Passage 3

Now read this passage. Think about the author's purpose as you read. When you finish, answer the questions that follow.

Beating Writer's Block

Imagine a boy sitting at his classroom desk, switching on an electronic word processor, or placing an empty pad of paper in front of him. He has at his disposal the instruments for writing—a pencil, pen, or a computer keyboard—and he is motivated to write, and yet he doesn't . . . or just can't.

The minutes tick by, and the boy stares at the empty paper or screen. He feels puzzled by his inability to organize his words and ideas, and then he becomes frustrated, which makes it even harder to think clearly. He jots down a few words and then, grumbling, erases them. Hours pass and he still hasn't accomplished anything.

Are you familiar with this sort of scenario? If you are, then you've experienced writer's block. This is a frustrating phenomenon that affects many potential writers. It restrains their creativity, keeps their productivity low, and generally makes writing a miserable chore. However, examining this confounding problem and some ways to reduce its effect on you can make writing enjoyable again.

Writer's block may have many easily understood causes, including tiredness or lack of fresh ideas. It may also have more underlying causes, like ugly emotions such as self-doubt. You may feel like you are incapable of writing anything valuable or that you could stare at the paper or screen for months without producing anything worthwhile. You may start to feel that writing is just not worth all the hassle.

Regardless of the cause, writer's block typically carries along feelings of panic, dissatisfaction, frustration, and additional self-doubt. Maybe the scariest thing about writer's block is that it seems to regenerate itself. The more blocked up your words are, the worse you feel about it—the worse you feel about it, the more your words block up!

So, your objective is to discover a method of breaking that gloomy cycle. Initially, you should think about other factors in your life that might be bothering you. These factors may be completely unrelated to writing (like failing a math test or arguing with a friend) that are clouding your thoughts. Working on a remedy to that concern may reduce your writer's block, as well as improve the rest of your daily life.

If the roots of your writer's block are simpler, then the solutions will likely also be simpler. There are dozens of fun, easy ways to kick writer's block out of your schedule!

Here's a scenario you may recognize: you have a writing assignment due early the next morning, but you haven't been able to get a grip on it yet. You're becoming frustrated and anxious as the hours pass but the paper remains empty. The first thing to do is remind yourself that negative feelings like frustration and anxiety are only going to add to your burden. When your brain is relaxed, you can then focus on getting your writing done right.

You've probably heard of "brainstorming," one useful tactic for dealing with writer's block. To brainstorm, just use a separate paper and scribble down whatever ideas come to mind. It may help to start by writing down your topic, and then making a simple diagram to show ideas related to that topic. If your topic was anacondas, you might write "anacondas" and then draw lines that connect concepts like "What they look like," "What they eat," "Where they live," and so on.

If you're capable of choosing or modifying your topic, be sure it's something you're interested in. You probably wouldn't be too enthusiastic about writing an essay on the history of socks! Choose something that excites your mind, because if you're excited about writing, the reader will likely be more excited to read.

Sometimes writer's block occurs because there are too many distractions around that interrupt your concentration. The distractions may be as elementary as a dripping faucet or the sound of voices upstairs, or more complicated, like worries over other obligations you may have. Whatever the distraction, it's not helping your writing. Try to always devote enough time for writing, and avoid noises or activities that can distract you. If you write with undivided attention, you'll likely finish sooner and have more time to focus on other concerns.

If a tight deadline isn't breathing down your neck, your options for beating writer's block are almost endless. Simply think of something that would relax you and clear out your brain. You can work on a separate project, take a walk, play a video game, watch a movie, read a chapter of a good book, or even take a nap. Some of these stress relievers may be just what you need to unclog your writer's block and let the words flow again.

Questions

1. The main purpose of this passage is to

    A   entertain readers with stories about writer's block
    B   convince readers that they can overcome writer's block
    C   describe to readers what it feels like to have writer's block
    D   inform readers about writer's block and how to overcome it

Tip

Go back and reread the article. What is its purpose?

2. The author would most likely agree that

    A   some people never experience writer's block
    B   good planning can help you avoid writer's block
    C   overconfidence is a common cause of writer's block
    D   stress has little to do with experiencing writer's block

Tip

Reread the passage and eliminate incorrect answer choices. Which answer choice is true based on the information in the passage.

3. Why does the author include the scenario of the boy staring at the blank page in the beginning of the passage? Use details and information from the passage in your answer.

    _____

    _____

    _____

Check your answers on the next page.

Passage 3: "Beating Writer's Block"

 Answers

1. D   The article is informative. It tells about writer's block and offers some suggestions for overcoming it. Answer choice D is the best answer.

2. B   The author says that writer's block can occur when you put off doing a writing assignment and it is due the next morning. Therefore, the author seems to believe that good planning might help you overcome writer's block. Answer choice B is the best answer.

3.   **Sample answer:** The scenario of the boy in the beginning is one that most of us can relate to, which is why the author includes it in the beginning of the passage. It is an effective lead-in to the rest of the passage.

Passage 4

Read this passage and answer the questions that follow.

Cutting Class Size

"Falling through the cracks" sounds like a scary prospect—and it is. For thousands of students in America, overcrowding in their schools is making their educational experience more straining and less effective. Promising students are falling through the cracks each day. They get lost in the crowd and never receive the individual attention and stimulation they need to reach their full potential.

Fortunately, there is a solution to this predicament. Reducing class size in America's schools is the best method by which we can eliminate these "cracks" in the educational system. This will be a challenging process, but many leading educators have developed a detailed plan to make it a reality.

The process should begin in the country's more troubled schools, in which the students' achievements have been consistently lower than average. These schools require special attention, and, by instituting small class size policies, they will receive it. The initial step would be to deliver adequate funding to these troubled schools, which will allow them to hire more well-qualified teachers and provide additional classroom space for the students. Once there is enough room to breathe, and enough concerned, properly trained teachers, the possibilities for the students are endless!

Classes of fifteen to twenty students would be ideal; the ratio of students per teacher would allow more individual attention for each student. Providing this reduced class size would greatly reduce many of the public's concerns about the U.S. educational system.

Students and parents alike have been worried by the sense of namelessness that exists in many modern schools. Under the current system, some students are just faces in a crowded classroom. If they aren't exceptional in an obvious way—such as being especially outgoing, academic, or athletic—they will likely be overlooked by their teachers and made to feel like nobodies. For instance, quiet students, no matter how talented they may be, are automatically at a big disadvantage. This is simply because they're harder to notice in a crowded room.

The namelessness problem is usually not a teacher's fault. Many teachers have to work with over a hundred different students per day, as well as manage troublemakers, do paperwork, and, of course, try their best to teach! It can be difficult to remember a hundred names, never mind any more personal details. And it can be impossible to notice small changes in individual students that might indicate more serious problems.

AUTHOR'S PURPOSE   Lesson 4

A reduction in class size could resolve these problems quickly. Teachers would have a much easier time getting to know their students, not just recognizing their faces. If a teacher knows a student's strengths and weaknesses, personality and interests, that can vastly improve a student's academic and personal experience. The teacher will be better able to help him or her, as well as communicate in more effective, meaningful ways.

For many students, the experience of attending overcrowded classes can be a miserable one. With thirty or more students confined in a small room, problems are inescapable. Even if everyone is cooperating, there will be some noise, confusion, and delays. If a student doesn't understand the material and would benefit from another explanation, he or she might be hesitant to ask the teacher for a recap because the remainder of the class might want to move on.

If everyone isn't cooperating, there can be chaos, like yelling, fighting, cheating—all manner of problems. It can make the classroom a stressful, depressing place to be. Students who are willing to follow the lesson are distracted and annoyed by other students. Students who don't want to follow the lesson can't be convinced to do so, because the teachers lack the time or resources to properly deal with them.

Smaller classes would eliminate these problems. With fewer students, there will almost certainly be reduced noise and distraction. A teacher will be able to guide the class much more easily, not having to shout over voices and spend valuable time trying to discipline troublemakers.

Of course, there are people opposed to the idea of reducing class sizes in America's schools. These critics mostly point to the problems of funding these significant changes. They are correct in that it would be a costly endeavor, but would it be worth the investment? Some critics have presented the challenge that small class size would not guarantee that the students will improve their performance in school. That may be true, but only because it depends on the students and their cooperation!

However, few could claim that the ideals of the small class size plan are deficient. A policy that allows students more access to instructors, and lets instructors become more familiar with students, promises to have a great positive effect on our nation's schools.

 Questions

1. Why did the author write this passage?

    A   to inform readers about class sizes in schools

    B   to teach readers how to reduce class sizes in schools

    C   to describe what it is like for a student in a large class

    D   to convince readers that smaller class sizes are needed

 Tip

What kind of language does the author use in this passage? What kind of article is it?

2. Which feature of small class size does the author value most?

    A   more personal attention
    B   more time for instruction
    C   less chaos in the classroom
    D   better cooperation from students

Tip

Consider how the author begins the passage. What feature of small class size is mentioned in the beginning and stressed throughout the article?

3. The author would most likely agree with which statement?

    A   Shy students might need extra attention.
    B   Small class size guarantees success in school.
    C   Talented students are better off in larger schools.
    D   Teachers should not be concerned with students' personal lives.

Tip

You might have to reread the article to eliminate incorrect answer choices.

4. Read these sentences from the introduction of the passage.

    "Falling through the cracks" sounds like a scary prospect—and it is. For thousands of students in America, overcrowding in their schools is making their education experience more straining and less effective.

Tip

Based on this sentence, what does the author want to show about children in over-crowded schools? Use details and information from the passage in your answer.

Check your answers on the next page.

Passage 4: "Cutting Class Size"

 Answers

1. **D** The author uses convincing language in this passage and presents an argument for smaller class size. Therefore, answer choice D is the correct answer.

2. **A** The author stresses that quiet students and those who are not gifted in some way are the most likely to remain nameless. The author stresses that smaller class sizes will give students much-needed personal attention from teachers. Answer choice A is the best answer.

3. **A** The author says that very quiet students are the most likely to fall through the cracks. The author would most likely believe that shy students might need extra attention. While answer choice B might also seem true, the author states in the passage that smaller class size does not guarantee success. Therefore, answer choice A is the correct answer.

4. **Sample answer:** The author is trying to show that some children are truly lost in the present educational system and have "fallen through the cracks," meaning no one is watching them or concerned with their learning. The author is trying to make the reader feel badly for these students and understand that something needs to be done.

Lesson 5: Literature, Part 1

Fiction

R8.B.1.1 **Interpret, compare, describe, analyze, and evaluate the components of fiction and literary nonfiction.**

- Explain, interpret, compare, describe, analyze, and/or evaluate character actions, motives, dialogue, emotions/feelings, traits, and relationships among characters within fictional and nonfictional text; explain, interpret, compare, describe, analyze, and/or evaluate the relationship between characters and other components of the text.

- Explain, interpret, compare, describe, analyze, and/or evaluate the setting of fiction or literary nonfiction; explain, interpret, compare, describe, analyze, and/or evaluate the relationship between setting and other components of text.

- Explain, interpret, compare, describe, analyze, and/or evaluate elements of the plot (conflict, rising action, climax, and/or resolution); explain, interpret, compare, describe, analyze, and/or evaluate the relationship between elements of the plot and other components of text.

- Explain, interpret, compare, describe, analyze, and/or evaluate the theme of fiction or literary nonfiction; explain, interpret, compare, describe, analyze, and/or evaluate the relationship between the theme and other components of text.

R8.B.1.2 **Make connections between texts.**

Questions about Literature, Part 1

Literary passages are fictional. For the PSSA, fictional passages may be short stories, poems, or excerpts from novels or short stories. Questions for literature assessment anchors on the PSSA often ask you about **characters.** You might be asked to choose a word that best describes a character. You might also be asked what a particular character might do in a given situation. You might also be asked about details related to the **plot,** what happens in a piece of writing and how problems or conflicts are resolved.

Some question on the PSSA will ask you to identify the **theme** of a passage, meaning you will have to indicate the overall message the author is trying to convey in the passage. Others will ask you about the **setting,** where and when a story or poem takes place.

Questions about literary passages might also ask you to identify the point of view and figurative language. You will learn about these types of question in the next lesson, Lesson 6, Literature, Part 2.

Activity 1

Read the following fable. Then write a brief character sketch of the fox. Consider what he is like and why he acts the way that he does.

The Fox and the Stork
(adapted from Aesop's Fables)

Once upon a time, the fox and the stork were friends. The fox invited the stork to dinner. He loved soup, so he placed soup on two shallow bowls on the table. The fox ate his soup, but the stork could not eat hers. She tried and tried, but could not get the soup out of the shallow bowl with her long, pointed beak. The stork tried to be polite to the fox, though, just in case he did not realize his error. The stork was very hungry, however, and eventually became angry. "I'm sorry the soup is not to your liking," the fox said.

"Oh, do not apologize," said the stork. "I hope you will return this visit and dine with me soon."

So the two chose a day and the fox visited the stork for dinner. The stork also served delicious soup, but in a very long-necked jar with a narrow mouth. The fox could not get the soup out of the jar. "I will not apologize for dinner," said the stork. "One bad turn deserves another."

_____

_____

_____

_____

Activity 2

Read the following fable. Then write a brief character sketch of the goat. Consider what he is like and where he went wrong.

The Fox and the Goat
(adapted from Aesop's Fables)

One day a fox fell deep into a well while trying to get a drink of water and could not get out again. He waited there until a thirsty goat came along to get a drink as well. The goat saw the fox at the bottom of the well and asked him how the water tasted.

"Oh, sir goat, this is the best water I've ever had!" shouted the Fox excitedly. "You simply must taste this water. You look very thirsty."

The goat grinned and nodded his head. He jumped down into the well, landing next to the fox, and started to drink. Now both animals were trapped in the well.

"How will we get out?" asked the goat nervously, for he was beginning to worry.

"If you put your feet on the wall and stretch up as far as you can," said the fox, "I'll climb up your back and then pull you out when I am at the top." The goat agreed, but once the fox was out, he kept running.

"Come back here!" cried the angry goat. "You broke your promise!"

"Yes, but you were foolish!" called the fox. "If you had not been thinking only about your thirst, you never would have been trapped to begin with. You should learn now to look before you leap!"

_____

_____

_____

_____

Passage 1

As you read the following passage, think about the narrator. What kind of person is she? When you finish reading, answer the questions that follow.

Excerpt from *Bleak House* (Chapter 3) by Charles Dickens

I have a great deal of difficulty in beginning to write my portion of these pages, for I know I am not clever. I always knew that. I can remember, when I was a very little girl indeed, I used to say to my doll, when we were alone together, "Now Dolly, I am not clever, you know very well, and you must be patient with me, like a dear!" And so she used to sit propped up in a great arm-chair, with her beautiful complexion and rosy lips, staring at me—or not so much at me, I think, as at nothing—while I busily stitched away, and told her every one of my secrets.

My dear old doll! I was such a little shy thing that I seldom dared to open my lips, and never dared to open my heart, to anybody else. It almost makes me cry to think what a relief it used to be to me, when I came home from school of a day, to turn up-stairs to my room, and say, "O you dear faithful Dolly, I knew you would be expecting me!" and then to sit down on the floor, leaning on the elbow of her great chair, and tell her all I had noticed since we parted. I had always rather a noticing way—not a quick way, O no!—a silent way of noticing what passed before me, and thinking I should like to understand it better. I have not by any means a quick understanding. When I love a person very tenderly indeed, it seems to brighten. But even that may be my vanity.

 Questions

1. Why did the narrator talk to her doll?

   _____

   _____

   _____

2. How does the narrator feel about her doll?

   _____

   _____

   _____

3. Why do you think the narrator doesn't like talking to other people?

_____

_____

_____

Check your answers on the next page.

Passage 1: Excerpt from "Bleak House"

 Answers

1. **Sample answer:** The narrator talked to her doll because she was shy and did not feel comfortable talking to other people. In school she was quiet and noticed things that she wanted to tell to someone, but she was afraid to open up to other people. When she got home, she told these things to her doll instead, and this made her feel better.

2. **Sample answer:** The narrator loves her doll and said it was a great relief to come home to it each day.

3. **Sample answer:** The narrator seems unsure of herself and has no confidence. As a girl, she was quiet because she was probably afraid that her peers would judge her negatively based on her stories and ideas. She tells the reader negative things about herself—she says she is not clever, she does not have a quick understanding, and she is vain—before the reader can make a negative judgment about her.

Passage 2

Read the following poem and answer the questions that follow. As you read, think about the message the author is trying to convey.

Up-Hill
by Christina Rossetti

Does the road wind up-hill all the way?
Yes, to the very end.
Will the day's journey take the whole long day?
From morn to night my friend.

But is there for the night a resting-place?
A roof for when the slow dark hours begin.
May not the darkness hide it from my face?
You cannot miss that inn.

Shall I meet other wayfarers at night?
Those who have gone before.
Then must I knock, or call when just in sight?
They will not keep you standing at that door.

Shall I find comfort, travel-sore and weak?
Or labour you shall find the sum.
Will there be beds for me and all who seek?
Yea, beds for all who come.

 Questions

1. How does the speaker of the poem feel about setting out on this journey?

    A curious
    B excited
    C regretful
    D miserable

 Tip

Reread the poem and consider the speaker's tone. What has the speaker done to let us know how she feels?

2.   What will happen when the author reaches the inn?

   A   She must knock on the door.
   B   She will be greeted and invited in to sleep.
   C   She will have to wait until morning for a bed.
   D   She must call out when she is close to the inn.

Tip

Reread the third stanza of the poem.

3.   Why do you think that all those who have come before are still at the inn? What does this say about the inn? Use details from the poem in your answer.

_____

_____

_____

Tip

Reread the poem several times. What type of journey leads a person to rest and never leave? What might the inn represent?

Check your answers on the next page.

Passage 2: "Up-Hill"

 Answers

1. A   The speaker's questions reveal that she is curious, but consider the other answer choices before choosing this answer. The speaker has done nothing to suggest that she is excited, and she does not seem regretful or miserable about the journey. The correct answer is A.

2. B   The speaker asks if she should knock or call out and is told that she will not be kept waiting at the door, meaning that neither action is necessary. Because she is told that she will not have to wait, answer choice C is incorrect. You can conclude that answer choice B is correct.

3.   **Sample answer:** All those who have come before are still at the inn because it represents a final resting place or destination. The author's journey is not an actual trip but a search for comfort from feeling "travel-sore and weak," or a rest after a long and hard life.

Passage 3

Read the following story. Think about Seth's problem as you read and how his outlook changes throughout the story. Then answer the questions that follow.

Mr. Salazar

Wearing new shorts and a new shirt and with his book bag on his back, Seth headed for the bus stop. *The first day of school is always a blast,* Seth thought. He couldn't wait to see some of his friends that he wasn't able to see over summer vacation while he worked with his grandfather on his peach farm.

Seth was certain that eighth grade was going to be his best year ever. As one of the oldest students, he knew just about everyone in the school. He was going to be on the varsity basketball team and might even be chosen as a starter. The best part was having Mr. Jordan as his homeroom teacher. Mr. Jordan had been Seth's English teacher for several years and Seth really enjoyed his classes, mainly because Mr. Jordan had a great sense of humor. He loved to laugh and he made learning new material great fun. After the class had read a new short story or novel, he would match students to characters and have them act out a chapter or two. While at first Seth thought this would be extremely corny and considered outright refusing to do it, he changed his mind when Mr. Jordan assigned him the part of an old woman in one of Flannery O'Connor's short stories. Seth tried in vain to raise his deep voice so it sounded like a woman's, but all he managed to do was squeak. The class was hysterical. Then Mr. Jordan assigned Seth's friend Charlie the part of a desk! Once everyone had their parts, they managed to get through it without laughing too loudly. Mr. Jordan discussed character motivation by asking each student (except Charlie) what made their character do the things that he or she did. Mr. Jordan was Seth's all-time favorite teacher.

That's why Seth was completely distraught to see another man standing in front of Mr. Jordan's desk. "Who's *that*?" he asked his friend Ashley. "And why is he in Mr. Jordan's classroom?" Ashley shook her head and told Seth she had no clue. The man was much younger than Mr. Jordan and, even though he hunched his shoulders and leaned forward slightly, he was extremely tall—too tall in Seth's opinion. The man slipped his hands into his pockets nervously and smiled an awkward, crooked smile. When Seth's eyes met his, he nodded, but Seth was too bewildered to respond.

When everyone entered the room the man introduced himself as Mr. Salazar. "Are you a substitute?" called out someone from the back of class.

"Nope. I'm going to be your teacher this year. Mr. Jordan and his wife relocated to New Jersey about a month ago. I was hired to take his place—and I'm honored to be your teacher this year."

Seth could not believe his ears. No more Mr. Jordan? That meant no more funny plays, no joking around in class—no more fun. This man looked serious, nervous, and too young to be a teacher. "Is this the first class you've ever taught?" Seth inquired.

Mr. Salazar laughed. "Yes," he replied. "I graduated college last May, but I student-taught during my last year. I'm going to teach you many new and interesting things and we're going to have lots of fun learning."

Yeah, right, Seth thought. *This is going to ruin everything.*

Seth and his friend Charlie made a beeline for the basketball court at recess. Seth was surprised to see Mr. Salazar on the court dribbling a basketball. His lanky frame moved surprisingly swiftly as he approached the hoop. He reached up and gently shot the ball—swish! Mr. Salazar stopped when he saw them. "Hey, boys. Would you like to play?" he asked.

Seth and Charlie approached him. Two other boys walked onto the court. "*You* play basketball?" Seth asked.

"You bet!" replied Mr. Salazar. "I played in both high school and college."

Seth caught the rebound and tried unsuccessfully to pass by Mr. Salazar. Seth laughed. "For a too-tall teacher, you can really move," he said. Mr. Salazar knocked the ball away from Seth and sunk it in the hoop. A crowd of students gathered around the court to watch Mr. Salazar play. The boys tried to beat him four to one, but it was no use. Exhausted, Seth plopped down on the side of the court. "You're so tall no one can beat you," Seth said.

"Nah," Mr. Salazar replied and sunk yet another basket. "Size doesn't have all that much to do with it. Some of the best players on my college team were only average height if not smaller. It's how you move that counts."

"Well, you sure can move," Seth said. "Could you teach us to move like that?"

"Sure!" said Mr. Salazar. "I'm going to teach you lots of things—and not just about basketball. We're going to start a new novel in English today. It's called *Dogsong*. Have you ever heard of it?"

Dogsong was written by Gary Paulsen, Seth's favorite author. Seth told Mr. Salazar about the other books he had read by Paulsen. When the bell rang ending recess, Seth headed back to class excitedly for the first time since he arrived at school. Maybe things weren't so bad after all.

 Questions

1. What does Seth think will be the best part of going back to school?

    A   He will be one of the oldest students.
    B   Mr. Jordan will be his homeroom teacher.
    C   He will be on the varsity basketball team.
    D   All of his friends will be back from summer vacation.

 Tip

Reread the first paragraph of the story. What is the main reason Seth is excited to go back to school?

2. The theme of this story can be best be stated as

   A   change is often a good thing
   B   surprises can sometimes be fun
   C   some people have a great deal in common
   D   things are not always as bad as they seem

Tip

Think about Seth. How does he feel in the beginning of the story? How does he feel at the end?

3. Which pair of words best describes Mr. Salazar?

   A   serious but nice
   B   nervous but tricky
   C   inexperienced but kind
   D   unsure but persistent

Tip

Eliminate the incorrect answer choices and then choose the one that best describes Mr. Salazar.

4. How does Seth's character change throughout the story? Use at least two details from the story to support your answer.

   _____

   _____

   _____

Tip

Reread the story. Note Seth's feelings as the story progresses.

Check your answers on the next page.

Passage 3: "Mr. Salazar"

 Answers

1. B In the beginning of the story, Seth thinks that the best part about going back to school will be having Mr. Jordan as a homeroom teacher. The correct answer is B.

2. D Seth is sad in the beginning of the story because his favorite teacher isn't there and he thinks that it's going to be a terrible year. But then he finds that he has things in common with his new teacher and his outlook improves. Answer choice D is the best answer.

3. C Mr. Salazar confesses that this is his first teaching job, so he is inexperienced. He seems very kind, however, and willing to try. Answer choice C is correct.

4. **Sample answer:** Seth starts out very excited about the start of the school year because he will have his favorite teacher, Mr. Jordan, as homeroom teacher. He is shocked to discover another man standing in front of Mr. Jordan's desk when he arrives at school. When he learns that this man is taking Mr. Jordan's place, he does not think much of him. He is young and awkward and Seth does not think he will be any good. Seth gets to know the new teacher better when he plays basketball with him, however, and his skill impresses Seth. Then he tells Seth they are going to read a book by Gary Paulsen, Seth's favorite author. Seth's mood improves a bit and he seems to be willing to give Mr. Salazar a chance.

Passage 4

Now read this passage and answer the questions that follow.

The Story of an Hour
by Kate Chopin

Knowing that Mrs. Mallard was afflicted with heart trouble, great care was taken to break to her as gently as possible the news of her husband's death.

It was her sister Josephine who told her, in broken sentences; veiled hints that revealed in half concealing. Her husband's friend Richards was there, too, near her. It was he who had been in the newspaper office when intelligence of the railroad disaster was received, with Brently Mallard's name leading the list of "killed." He had only taken the time to assure himself of its truth by a second telegram, and had hastened to forestall any less careful, less tender friend in bearing the sad message.

She did not hear the story as many women have heard the same, with a paralyzed inability to accept its significance. She wept at once, with sudden, wild abandonment, in her sister's arms. When the storm of grief had spent itself she went away to her room alone. She would have no one follow her.

There stood, facing the open window, a comfortable, roomy armchair. Into this she sank, pressed down by a physical exhaustion that haunted her body and seemed to reach into her soul.

She could see in the open square before her house the tops of trees that were all aquiver with the new spring life. The delicious breath of rain was in the air. In the street below a peddler was crying his wares. The notes of a distant song which some one was singing reached her faintly, and countless sparrows were twittering in the eaves.

There were patches of blue sky showing here and there through the clouds that had met and piled one above the other in the west facing her window.

She sat with her head thrown back upon the cushion of the chair, quite motionless, except when a sob came up into her throat and shook her, as a child who has cried itself to sleep continues to sob in its dreams.

She was young, with a fair, calm face, whose lines bespoke repression and even a certain strength. But now there was a dull stare in her eyes, whose gaze was fixed away off yonder on one of those patches of blue sky. It was not a glance of reflection, but rather indicated a suspension of intelligent thought.

There was something coming to her and she was waiting for it, fearfully. What was it? She did not know; it was too subtle and elusive to name. But she felt it, creeping out of the sky, reaching toward her through the sounds, the scents, the color that filled the air.

Now her bosom rose and fell tumultuously. She was beginning to recognize this thing that was approaching to possess her, and she was striving to beat it back with her will—as powerless as her two white slender hands would have been. When she abandoned herself a little whispered word escaped her slightly parted lips. She said it over and over under her breath: "free, free, free!" The vacant stare and the look of terror that had followed it went from her eyes. They stayed keen and bright. Her pulses beat fast, and the coursing blood warmed and relaxed every inch of her body.

She did not stop to ask if it were or were not a monstrous joy that held her. A clear and exalted perception enabled her to dismiss the suggestion as trivial. She knew that she would weep again when she saw the kind, tender hands folded in death; the face that had never looked save with love upon her, fixed and gray and dead. But she saw beyond that bitter moment a long procession of years to come that would belong to her absolutely. And she opened and spread her arms out to them in welcome.

There would be no one to live for during those coming years; she would live for herself. There would be no powerful will bending hers in that blind persistence with which men and women believe they have a right to impose a private will upon a fellow-creature. A kind intention or a cruel intention made the act seem no less a crime as she looked upon it in that brief moment of illumination.

And yet she had loved him—sometimes. Often she had not. What did it matter! What could love, the unsolved mystery, count for in the face of this possession of self-assertion which she suddenly recognized as the strongest impulse of her being!

"Free! Body and soul free!" she kept whispering.

Josephine was kneeling before the closed door with her lips to the keyhold, imploring for admission. "Louise, open the door! I beg; open the door—you will make yourself ill. What are you doing, Louise? For heaven's sake open the door."

"Go away. I am not making myself ill." No; she was drinking in a very elixir of life through that open window.

Her fancy was running riot along those days ahead of her. Spring days, and summer days, and all sorts of days that would be her own. She breathed a quick prayer that life might be long. It was only yesterday she had thought with a shudder that life might be long.

She arose at length and opened the door to her sister's importunities. There was a feverish triumph in her eyes, and she carried herself unwittingly like a goddess of Victory. She clasped her sister's waist, and together they descended the stairs. Richards stood waiting for them at the bottom.

Some one was opening the front door with a latchkey. It was Brently Mallard who entered, a little travel-stained, composedly carrying his grip-sack and umbrella. He had been far from the scene of the accident, and did not even know there had been one. He stood amazed at Josephine's piercing cry; at Richards' quick motion to screen him from the view of his wife.

But Richards was too late.

When the doctors came, they said she had died of heart disease—of the joy that kills.

Questions

1. Which word best describes Mrs. Mallard when she imagines life after her husband's death?

    A   sad
    B   angry
    C   unsure
    D   excited

 Tip

The story says that Mrs. Mallard wept at once when she learns of her husband's death. How does she feel after this?

2. Why does Richards try to screen Mrs. Mallard from the sight of her husband?

    A   He knows she will feel confused.
    B   He knows she does not want to see him.
    C   He is not sure if it is really Brently Mallard.
    D   He thinks she will be so happy she will be sick.

 Tip

What is wrong with Josephine Mallard? Why do people take care when telling her of very bad—or very good—things?

3. What killed Mrs. Mallard? Use details in the story to support your answer.

    _____

    _____

    _____

 Tip

Reread the last line of the story. Why does Mrs. Mallard die?

Check your answers on the next page.

Passage 4: "The Story of an Hour"

 Answers

1.   D   Mrs. Mallard is thrilled when she imagines a life where she is unmarried and free. Answer choice D is the best answer.

2.   D   Richards tries to shield Mrs. Mallard from the sight of her husband because he thinks that she will be instantly happy and the shock might be too much for her. Answer choice D is the best answer.

3.   **Sample answer:** Mrs. Mallard dies because she is unhappy that her husband is alive. She has just imagined a life without him and she is very excited by this. Since he is alive, she will continue to be married and live the same life that she has been living. It is ironic because everyone thinks her shock is happiness when, in fact, it is sadness.

Lesson 6: Literature, Part 2

R8.B.2.1   **Identify, interpret, describe, and analyze figurative language in fiction and nonfiction.**

- Identify, explain, interpret, describe, and/or analyze examples of personification, simile, metaphor, hyperbole, and imagery in text.

- Identify, explain, interpret, describe, and/or analyze the author's purpose for and effectiveness at using figurative language in text.

R8.B.2.2   **Identify, interpret, describe, and analyze the point of view of the narrator in fictional and nonfictional text.**

- Identify, explain, interpret, describe, and/or analyze point of view of the narrator as first person or third person point of view.

- Explain, interpret, describe, and/or analyze the effectiveness of the point of view used by the author.

Questions about Literature, Part 2

In the last lesson, you answered questions about some aspects of literature including character, theme, plot, and setting. In this lesson, you will answer questions about figurative language and point of view.

Figurative language is language that is not literal. Similes and metaphors are examples of **figurative language**, as are personification, hyperbole, and imagery.

You will also be asked questions on the PSSA about **point of view**. Sometimes you will have to identify whether a passage is written in first or third person. Other times, you will have to name the narrator in the story.

Activity

Rewrite each of the following sentences so that they are literal instead of figurative.

My lawyer is a shark.

_____

I have a few tricks up my sleeve.

_____

My sister let the cat out of the bag about the surprise party.

I have to study tonight, so I'll take a rain check on dinner.

My friend Gina is a doll.

I would give my right arm for a new set of golf clubs.

Passage 1

Read the following passage and then answer the questions that follow.

Memories of Montgomery
by Evelyn Smith

Growing up as a black child in Montgomery, Alabama, in the 1950s was challenging, and it taught me some valuable lessons. Unfortunately, most lessons learned during this time were taught the hard way, which seemed to be the only way. During the earliest part of my childhood, most whites in Montgomery essentially pretended that my family and others like us did not exist. We sat in the rear of the bus, did not dine in restaurants, and occupied separate waiting rooms everywhere we went. As a child I did not question these practices because I had never yearned for an equal world. My parents, however, longed for things to improve.

It was December 1, 1955—I was six—when a woman named Rosa Parks refused to give up her seat to a white man on a Montgomery bus. Suddenly, my parents would no longer allow us to travel on Montgomery public transportation. I didn't understand the reasoning behind it, but I knew that racial conflict in Montgomery was getting severe. Our pastor, Pastor Vernon, organized a car pool for the blacks in our neighborhood so that we wouldn't have to furnish money to the city by using public transportation. One day, on our way to school, an enraged white man smashed the car's windshield with the tip of his

cane. I was never so frightened, and that was when I realized the consuming nature of foolish hatred—his, not my own. A week later, after my mother started to walk me to school, Pastor Vernon was arrested while driving that same car. The officers said he was speeding, but Pastor Vernon insisted that he wasn't, and I knew that he wouldn't lie.

All through that winter I walked to school, ignoring the glares of the whites as we passed, playing word games with my mother to forget about hatred, about the reasons we were walking, the reasons I was beginning to understand. When my mother read of bombings and riots in the paper she would let me stay home from school. At first this was bells and whistles to me, but then I began to recognize the terror in my mother's eyes, and I felt like a prisoner, wondering if I would ever ride the bus again. Then, on November 13, 1956, the Supreme Court ruled that segregation on public buses in Montgomery was illegal. On my eighth birthday, my mother and I sat directly behind the driver, and though the dangers were not over, this was a very happy memory for me because it was the first time I felt like we were winning against hate.

 Questions

1. What point of view is this story written in?

   _____

2. If the point of view were changed, how would the story be different?

   _____

   _____

3. Read this sentence from the passage. Underline the metaphor once. Under the simile twice.

   At first this was bells and whistles to me, but then I began to recognize the terror in my mother's eyes, and I felt like a prisoner, wondering if I would ever ride the bus again.

   Check your answers on the next page.

Passage 1: "Memories of Montgomery"

 Answers

1. This story is written in the first person.

2. **Sample answer:** If the story were written in the third person, it would not be as personal—it might not be as clear how the character felt.

3. At first this was <u>bells and whistles</u> to me, but then I began to recognize the terror in my mother's eyes, and I felt <u>like a prisoner</u>, wondering if I would ever ride the bus again.

Passage 2

Read this passage and answer the questions that follow.

The Bunkhouse

Alejandro and Jerry planned to build the best bunkhouse anyone had ever seen. They had built a bunkhouse several years ago, but that one had been shoddy and unsophisticated—"very childish," was how Jerry described it. They'd used old, knotted wood that looked as if they had excavated it from a junk pile, and hammered it together clumsily. Now that they were older and more knowledgeable, they knew they could do better.

The friends decided to build the bunkhouse in a vacant yard behind their apartment building and had obtained permission from Mr. Fernando, the owner of their apartment building and the land.

"If we start now, we can finish in a day or so," Jerry concluded enthusiastically.

"No way," Alejandro protested. "Remember how we rushed to build the last bunkhouse and how badly it turned out? We need to go back to square one." Alejandro suggested dedicating more time to this latest endeavor to make it a castle. Jerry considered this idea and then agreed. "Now that that's resolved," said Alejandro, "let's split up and gather the materials we'll need."

When they returned, they noticed a major disparity between the types of materials they had brought. Alejandro had brought library books on how to install running water, lights—even air conditioning. Jerry, on the other hand, had brought a pile of old knotted wood from a junk pile. Alejandro accused Jerry of being sloppy, and Jerry accused Alejandro of being unrealistic.

"Don't you want to make the best bunkhouse we can?" Alejandro demanded.

"Don't you want to make something instead of reading all day?" Jerry countered.

When they tired of arguing, they devised a plan that satisfied them both. They would do some reading, but they would also put the wood to use. They worked together to construct two benches from the wood, and built a simple canopy to keep the hot sun out. Then they relaxed on the benches and read the library books. There they sat for many pleasant hours, planning the ideal bunkhouse they would build another day.

 Questions

1. Which of the following is an example of a metaphor?

   A "No way," Alejandro protested.
   B We need to go back to square one.
   C Alejandro accused Jerry of being sloppy, and Jerry accused Alejandro of being unrealistic.
   D They had built a bunkhouse several years ago, but that one had been shoddy and unsophisticated—"very childish," was how Jerry described it.

 Tip

Remember that a metaphor compares two things without using "like" or "as."

2. This passage is told from the point of view of which character?

   A Jerry
   B Alejandro
   C Mr. Fernando
   D someone not in the story

 Tip

Think about what person this story is told. Who is speaking? What do you know about the speaker?

Now check your answers on the next page. Read the explanations after each answer.

Passage 2: "The Bunkhouse"

 Answers

1. B   "We need to go back to square one" is a metaphor meaning, "We need to go back to the beginning." Answer choice B is correct.

2. D   This passage is told by a narrator who is not involved in the story. It is written in the third person.

Passage 3

Read the following passage and answer the questions that follow.

Bitter Competition

Sarah Kowalski and Rosa Lee had been best friends since they were very young. They grew up in the same neighborhood, played in the same playgrounds, and attended the same school. They were like bookends. However, there was a unique component to their friendship—they found themselves constantly in competition.

For a while, the competitiveness enhanced their friendship. They enjoyed playing chess to determine which of them could outsmart and outmaneuver the other. Whenever they participated in sports, they played on opposing teams in order to determine who could pitch, catch, or throw with the greatest skill. In the classroom they routinely compared their test scores and strived to outdo one another every time a math or science test rolled around.

The Lee and Kowalski families were pleased because the competition appeared to make their daughters thrive. Both girls were honor-roll students who excelled in athletics. What the families failed to comprehend was that both Sarah and Rosa often got frustrated by their inability to get an upper hand in their contests and that this frustration was beginning to take its toll on their friendship.

One morning, the girls discovered that there was an important midterm exam approaching in their Algebra I class. Sarah was distressed about that because algebra was her weak spot. She just couldn't grasp the concept of replacing numbers with letters. Worst of all, she knew that Rosa was proficient at algebra and might take an overwhelming lead in their contests. Sarah was determined to put an end to Rosa's winning streak.

Sarah began studying diligently for the algebra exam a week in advance. Although she felt resolved, she was still having difficulty with the material and the extra pressure of the competition was driving her crazy. The night before the exam, Sarah disappeared into her room to try to memorize all she could. She recited, "The FOIL method—multiply the First term, then the Outer, then the Inner, then the Last. First, Outer, Inner, Last—that spells FOIL." Then she closed the book and recited it from memory. She was thrilled that she had absorbed some information, and thought maybe her cause wasn't so hopeless after all.

The next morning, Sarah watched anxiously as her algebra teacher passed out the exam. She wanted to get the paper in her hands as soon as possible. Otherwise, she feared, she would forget what she had memorized. As soon as the exam was on her desk, she hunched over it and began scanning it—most of the questions dealt with the FOIL method, as she had anticipated. As soon as she began to write, though, her mind went blank. She couldn't recollect what the letters in FOIL represented.

Sarah tried to stay relaxed, but then she glanced over at Rosa, who was jotting down numbers and equations rapidly. To Rosa, the exam was a breeze! Seeing this made Sarah even more uncomfortable and made her memory even worse. Did the F in FOIL stand for "front," "fraction," "first," "furthest"— or "failure"?

Before she knew it, the class was over and she had no alternative but to submit the exam with only a few questions answered. The next day she was disappointed, but not surprised, to see that she had failed the exam miserably. After class, Rosa approached her, smiling broadly. "I got a 97 on that one. What a piece of cake!"

Suddenly Sarah felt furious, and vented her frustration on Rosa. "So what? Big deal—you're better at math than I am and you got a better grade. Well, who cares?"

Rosa was speechless.

"I got a 46," Sarah announced. "And it's partially your fault. I was looking at you writing so quickly and I was so worried about our stupid competitions that I couldn't even remember what FOIL stands for."

Rosa's eyes filled with tears. "Sarah, I'm really sorry," she said, suddenly awakening to the realization that she and Sarah were now more competitors than friends. "I feel awful about your grade, really I do. I'm certain we could work this problem out if we discuss it maturely." Despite Rosa's plea, Sarah spun around and stormed away.

Later in the day, Rosa approached Sarah again. "Sarah, please forgive me. I'm sorry I didn't see how upset you were. You're my best friend—I don't know what I would do without you," she pleaded.

Sarah smiled, though it was a dejected smile. It seemed that she had redirected her anger at herself. "It's okay, Rosa," she said. "Don't worry about it. I'm just a really poor student, and you're better than me, that's all."

"No, I'm not!" Rosa countered. "You just messed up this one time. How about we study for the next test together? This way we'll both be winners—and no more contests. If I lose your friendship, I will be the biggest loser ever!"

Sarah hugged Rosa and accepted Rosa's offer to study together. They promised that from now on they would help each other instead of competing against each other.

 Questions

1. Which of the following is an example of a simile?

   A   "What a piece of cake!"
   B   They were like bookends.
   C   Sarah was determined to put an end to Rosa's winning streak.
   D   Sarah was distressed because algebra was her weak spot.

 Tip

Which answer choice makes a comparison using "like" or "as"?

2. Read the sentence below.

   To Rosa, the exam was a breeze!

   This sentence is an example of

   A   a simile
   B   hyperbole
   C   a metaphor
   D   personification

 Tip

Think about the definition of each type of speech. Then choose the answer choice that best fits.

3. How do you think the story would change if was written from Sarah's point of view? Use two examples from the story to support your answer.

 Tip

Think about how Sarah felt when she could not remember the FOIL method.

Check your answers on the next page.

Passage 3: "Bitter Competition"

 Answers

1. B   "They were like bookends" is a simile because it's a comparison joined by "like." Answer choice B is correct.

2. C   The sentence shown is a metaphor; a comparison without "like" or "as."

3.   **Sample answer:** If the story were written from Sarah's point of view, we might better understand Sarah's feelings. She would express more anger at Rosa breezing through the math exam and she might even reveal how she feels about their competition.

Passage 4

Read the following passage and answer the questions that follow.

Because I Could Not Stop for Death
Emily Dickinson

Because I could not stop for Death—
He kindly stopped for me—
The Carriage held but just Ourselves—
And Immortality.

We slowly drove—He knew no haste
And I had put away
My labor and my leisure too,
For His Civility—

We passed the School, where Children strove
At Recess—in the Ring—
We passed the Fields of Gazing Grain—
We passed the Setting Sun—

Or rather—He passed us—
The Dews drew quivering and chill—
For only Gossamer, my Gown—
My Tippet—only Tulle—

We paused before a House that seemed
A Swelling of the Ground—
The Roof was scarcely visible—
The Cornice—in the Ground—

Since then—'tis Centuries—and yet
Feels shorter than the Day
I first surmised the Horses' Heads
Were toward Eternity—

 Questions

1. Read these lines from the poem.

    Because I could not stop for Death—
    He kindly stopped for me—

    What type of figurative language is used here?

    A   a simile
    B   hyperbole
    C   a metaphor
    D   personification

 Tip

Think about the definition of each type of language. Then choose the correct answer.

2. This poem is written from which point of view?

    A   first person
    B   second person
    C   third person
    D   omniscient

 Tip

Reread the beginning of the poem for a clue.

3. What are some possible metaphors in the poem? Use two examples to support your answer.

    _____

    _____

    _____

 Tip

Reread the poem. Which things might stand for something else?

Check your answers on the next page.

Passage 4: "Because I Could Not Stop for Death"

 Answers

1. D   The speaker of the poem personifies death. Answer choice D is correct.

2. A   The speaker of the poem speaks in the first person; she uses "I." Answer choice A is correct.

3.   **Sample answer:** In the third stanza of the poem, the school, fields of grain, and setting sun might be metaphors for the stages of the poet's life: her childhood, adulthood, and old age. The house she refers to might be her tombstone.

PART 2:
Writing and Revising

In this part of this book, you will learn how to prepare for the PSSA Writing test. This test contains two parts. For the first part of the PSSA Writing test, you will read several passages, which are drafts of essays, articles, or letters. You will answer multiple-choice questions asking you to choose the best way to fix some of these errors. On the actual test, you will complete two sessions containing these types of essays and questions. They will account for 20 percent of your grade on the writing test.

For the second part, you will be asked to write two essays in response to writing prompts. One of these prompts will be informational, meaning it may ask you to describe or explain something. The other prompt will be persuasive. For persuasive essays, you will need to convince the reader to believe as you believe. The essays you write will make up 80 percent of your grade on the writing test. You will have 60 minutes to respond to each prompt.

You will learn about the revising and editing portion of the PSSA Writing test in Lesson 1. You will learn about the PSSA Writing essay portion of the test in Lesson 2 of this section, in which you will also learn how these essays are graded.

Lesson 1: Revising/Editing

This lesson covers the following skill for revising (1.5.8.E and 1.5.8.F): revise your essay to ensure that it:

- Has good opening and closing sentences
- Contains an introduction, a body, and a conclusion
- Stays focused on the task
- Is organized effectively
- Uses correct grammar, spelling, and punctuation
- Contains good sentence construction
- Uses a variety of verbs

On the PSSA Writing test, you will be asked some multiple-choice questions about passages containing errors. For example, you may be asked to choose the best way to combine two sentences or to eliminate a grammatical error in a sentence. Other questions will ask you to choose the correct pronoun or verb in a sentence or which sentence should be deleted from a paragraph. Each sentence in these passages will be numbered.

Sample Passage and Multiple-Choice Questions

The letter below is a draft that Jack wrote to the editor of a newspaper. The letter contains errors. Read the letter to answer questions 1–3.

Dear Editer,

1 Last week, I was disgusted by the aloominum cans, coffee cups, newspapers, and food wrappers that litered the ground at Newbury Public Park. **2** More disturbing than the heaps of garbage, however, _____ the woman who finished her diet soda. **3** And tossed the can too the ground. **4** she threw her trash on the ground, rather than walk fifteen feet to the nearest receptacle. **5** I have to wonder if this lady throws garbage on the floor of her home? **6** Why does she think that its acceptable to do so in a public place? **7** I used to spend a lot of time playing in the park when I was younger.

8 I strongly erge city council to do something about this problem. **9** Newbury Public Park use to be one of best parts of town and now thanks to people like the diet soda woman. **10** It has become a garbage dump Otherwise Newbury public park will soon be newbury Public Dump.

Sincerely,
Jack Chaucer

Questions

1.　Which sentence should the writer remove from the passage because it is not relevant to the topic?

 A sentence 3
 B sentence 5
 C sentence 7
 D sentence 8

Tip
Choose the sentence that is *not* related to the main idea of the letter.

2.　Choose the correct form of the word to fill in the blank in sentence 2.

More disturbing than the heaps of garbage, however, _____ the woman who finished her diet soda and tossed the can to the ground.

 A was
 B were
 C has been
 D will be

Tip
Remember that the word "woman" is singular.

3.　Which word is spelled incorrectly?

 A <u>disgusted</u> in sentence 1
 B <u>heaps</u> in sentence 2
 C <u>receptacle</u> in sentence 4
 D <u>acceptible</u> in sentence 6

Tip
Sometimes writing down a word can help you determine if it is spelled incorrectly.

Check your answers on the next page.

REVISING/EDITING

Lesson 1

 Answers

1. C   Sentence 7 says that the author used to spend time playing in the park. This is not related to the main idea of the letter.

2. A   A singular subject requires a singular verb. Answer choice A is the correct answer.

3. D   Acceptable is spelled with *-able*.

Lesson 2: Essay Writing

This lesson covers the following skills for writing (1.4.8.B and 1.4.8.C): writing a first draft of an essay in response to a writing prompt that:

- Is clearly organized

- Has a focus

- Includes adequate supporting details

- Uses appropriate language

PSSA Writing Prompts

You will learn how to write essays that respond to a writing prompt. These are essays for which you should do some prewriting, drafting, and revising. On the PSSA, you will be asked to respond to either an expository or a persuasive writing prompt. You will have about 40 minutes to complete this task.

- **Informational Prompt**—An informational prompt defines, explains, or tells how to do something. The following is an example of an informational writing prompt:

   Write an essay that explains the qualities a special place should possess.

- **Persuasive Prompt**—A persuasive prompt convinces the reader to accept your opinion or to take a specific action. The following is an example of a persuasive writing prompt:

   To cut back on expenses, your principal has asked the school board for permission to cancel all field trips for the remainder of the year. Some parents think this is a good idea because they consider field trips "vacations" from learning and, therefore, an unnecessary expense.

   Write a letter to the school board explaining your position on the issue. Use facts and examples to develop your argument.

   For the PSSA Writing essay test, you will use scratch paper to organize your thoughts. Then you will write your response in your test booklet.

Developing Your Essays: The Three Stages of Writing

As you begin to develop your essay, you should follow the three stages of writing: prewriting, drafting, and **revising**. On the PSSA you will be asked to respond to either an informational prompt or a persuasive writing prompt. For either type of writing prompt, you should always begin to develop your essay by prewriting.

Prewriting—RECORD Your Ideas

The main purpose of prewriting is to record your ideas. You can do this by brainstorming what you will be writing about in your essay. Start by jotting down ideas and possible angles for your essay. Think about the positive and negative aspects of a topic. Think about the audience for whom you will be writing and the purpose of your writing. Are you writing to entertain readers with a story, give your opinion, or explain something? Once you have determined your central idea, purpose, and audience, write down some supporting material and organize or outline your ideas into a logical sequence.

Suppose your task is to write an essay in support of or against tearing down an old building:

> At the last city council meeting, a local business owner asked the council members for permission to tear down a historic building on Main Street to build a new clothing store in its place. Council members were divided on the issue. Some argued that the building was built before the Civil War and had too much historic value to be destroyed. Others argued that the old building was nothing more than an eyesore and a safety hazard and that a new store would make the downtown area more attractive.
>
> The mayor decided to postpone voting on the issue until she could hear more details about both sides of the issue. How do you feel about tearing down the historic building?
>
> Write an essay giving your opinion on the issue. Use facts and examples to develop your argument.

How would you begin to prepare an essay on this issue? First, you would take a moment to jot down a few notes about the issue. Why is the old building important? What are the benefits of the new store? You would ask yourself how you feel about the issue. Do you disagree with tearing down the building or would you rather have a new clothing store? Once you decide on the angle you want to take in your essay, add some details to support your position. You could create a web to help develop your argument and organize your ideas.

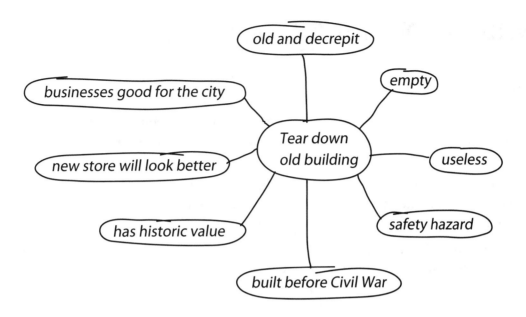

Prewriting— EVALUATE Your Ideas

When you have finished developing your argument, evaluate what you've written. Which ideas will help persuade the reader to share your opinion? Which ideas might weaken your argument? Don't be afraid to eliminate one or more of your ideas.

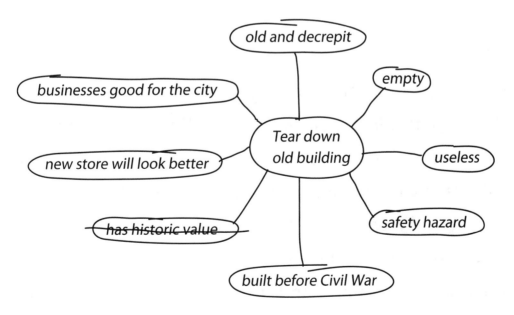

The fact that the building has historic value doesn't support the argument to tear it down. You probably wouldn't want to focus your essay on the historic value of the building if you were trying to convince readers to tear it down.

Prewriting—ORGANIZE Your Ideas

A good essay is organized into three parts:

1. Introduction—An essay should always begin with an introduction. The introduction should give readers a good idea of what to expect in the essay and give them a clue as to why you are writing the essay.

2. Body—The body of the essay is where you present the main ideas of the essay. Your main ideas, or, in this example, your main arguments, should be clearly explained. State your main ideas or opinions and support them with details.

3. Conclusion—The conclusion should provide a quick summary of your essay and leave the reader with your final word on the issue.

Drafting—Begin Your FIRST DRAFT

In the drafting stage of writing, you will write a rough draft of your work. An important thing to remember when writing your draft is to get your ideas down on paper. In this stage of writing, your writing does not have to be perfect. It is acceptable for the rough draft to have mistakes in grammar, spelling, and punctuation. These mistakes can be changed or fixed later.

Your first draft may look something like this:

> I think that replacing the building with a new clothing store is a grate idea. At the last city council meeting a local business owner asked permishon to tear down the old building on Main St. The business owner wants to build a new clothing store in its place. I think city council should vote for this project.
>
> Right now, the old building is full of broke windows. The doors are missing and bats and rats live their. More than anything, the building is an eye sore. A new building of any kind would look better.

Some city council members have argued that the old building is historic. Because it was built before the civil war. But, they fail to mention that the building has is in disrepare. Building a new store will improve the look of the downtown area. Pieces of broken glass and brick could easily fall to the ground and hurt people on the sidewalk the building is just not safe.

Finally, the old building is empty and useless. Bilding a new store in it's place would bring more people and more money into the city. It's taking up a lot of space and it's not being used for anything.

I would like to ask all city council members to think about how wonderful Main St. could look if the unsafe, useless, eyesore of a building was torn down. And replaced with a brand new store.

Revising and Editing—Preparing the FINAL DRAFT

After you write your rough draft, it's time to begin revising and editing your work. Read your rough draft carefully. Look for mistakes in grammar, spelling, punctuation, and capitalization. Look for sentence fragments. Make sure that you have stated your main idea or that you have provided enough supporting details for readers to determine the central theme. Reword sentences or move entire paragraphs to make your writing flow in a clear, logical order. Add more details to make your writing vibrant and exciting.

Editorial Symbols

When you edit your first draft, you will find it helpful to use editorial symbols. These are marks on the page that show how you want your composition to be improved. Here are the most common editorial symbols:

⨎	This is a delete symbol. It tells you what should be removed from the text.
∧	This is an insert symbol. It tells you what should be added to the text.
⊙	This symbol tells you to add a period.
≡	This mark under a letter means that it should be changed to an uppercase letter.
/	This mark through a letter tells you that it should be changed to a lowercase letter.
⌒	This symbol means that you should delete a word or space and bring the surrounding letters together.

When you have finished revising your first draft, refer to the Writer's Checklist to help perfect your essay. Make sure that your essay hits each point listed in the following Writer's Checklist. Then write the final copy of your work in the answer booklet of your test.

Writer's Checklist

_____ Focus on the main idea of your writing and think about your audience.

_____ Support your main idea with interesting facts and details.

_____ Organize your ideas in a logical sequence that best communicates what you are trying to say.

_____ Vary the length and structure of your sentences.

_____ Know the meanings of the words you choose, and use them correctly.

_____ Check the basics. Make sure your capitalization, punctuation, and spelling are correct.

_____ Use your best handwriting for the final copy of your writing.

The final draft of your essay might look something like this:

At the last city council meeting, a local business owner asked permission to tear down the old building on Main Street and construct a new clothing store in its place. I think that replacing the old, rundown building with a new clothing store is a great idea. I encourage city council to vote in favor of this project.

Some city council members have argued that the old building holds a lot of historic value because it was built before the Civil War. However, they fail to mention that the building has fallen into a state of disrepair. Pieces of broken glass and brick could easily fall to the ground and hurt people on the sidewalk. The building is just not safe.

Replacing the old building with a new store will improve the appearance of the downtown area. Right now, the old building is full of broken windows. The doors are missing and it's home to many bats and rats. More than anything, the building is an eyesore. A new building of any kind would be an improvement.

Finally, the old building is empty and useless. It's taking up a lot of valuable property and not being used for anything. Building a new store in its place would bring more people and more money into the city.

In conclusion, I would like to encourage all city council members to think about how wonderful Main Street could look if an unsafe, useless, eyesore of a building was removed and replaced with a brand new store.

In order to achieve the highest score for your essay, make sure that you use the three stages of writing and the Writer's Checklist. Also, pay attention to the content and organization of your essay, as well as usage, sentence construction, and mechanics.

Content/Organization

As mentioned earlier, your essay should be framed by strong opening and closing ideas. Make sure that you have addressed reasons that your issue is important. Conclude by stating why you feel as you do.

In between the opening and closing of your essay are your main ideas. Make sure that your ideas are clear, and that you have included a variety of main ideas and have not simply stressed the same point multiple times. Your ideas should follow a logical progression, meaning that transition from one main idea to another should not be choppy, but instead should flow easily from one idea to the next. Your ideas should also be supported by details, or reasons why you believe your ideas to be true. Also, be sure that your transitions from the introduction to the body to the conclusion are fluid instead of choppy.

Sentence Construction

Make sure that you follow traditional grammar rules when composing sentences. You should check to make sure that you have placed periods and commas in logical places. Make sure that you vary the length and structure of your sentences. This will help to improve your composition.

Usage

When you revise and edit, make sure that you use correct verb tense and agreement. For example, if you are using past tense verbs to describe something that happened in the past, then make sure that all the verbs describing this past event are in the past tense. Also, look at your pronouns (*I, you, he, she, it, we, they*) to make sure that you have used them correctly. Examine your essay to make sure you have used words that will engage the reader. If you don't like the look or sound of a certain word in your essay, try to replace it with a better one.

Mechanics

Mechanics are the spelling, capitalization, and punctuation in your essay. You are not allowed to use a dictionary during the test, so try to do your best with spelling and capitalization. Using precise spelling, capitalization, and punctuation will make it easier for people to read and understand your essay.

How Essays Are Graded

Written responses on the PSSA are scored using a four-point scale. Each essay is scored twice, one for composition and once for conventions.

Informational Essays

Informational essays are scored using the following rubric:

4 *Focus*
Sharp, distinct controlling point made about a single topic with evident awareness of task and audience.

Content Development
Substantial, relevant, and illustrative content that demonstrates a clear understanding of the purpose. Thorough elaboration with effectively presented information consistently supported with well-chosen details.

Organization
Effective organizational strategies and structures, such as logical order and transitions, which develop a controlling idea.

Style
Precise control of language, stylistic techniques, and sentence structures that creates a consistent and effective tone.

3 *Focus*
Clear controlling point made about a single topic with general awareness of task and audience.

Content Development
Adequate, specific, and/or illustrative content that demonstrates an understanding of the purpose. Sufficient elaboration with clearly presented information supported with well-chosen details.

Organization
Organizational strategies and structures, such as logical order and transitions, which develop a controlling idea.

Style
Appropriate control of language, stylistic techniques, and sentence structures that creates a consistent tone.

2 *Focus*
Vague evidence of a controlling point made about a single topic with an inconsistent awareness of task and audience.

Content Development
Inadequate, vague content that demonstrates a weak understanding of the purpose. Underdeveloped and/or repetitive elaboration with inconsistently supported information. May be an extended list.

Organization

Inconsistent organizational strategies and structures, such as logical order and transitions, which ineffectively develop a controlling idea.

Style

Limited control of language and sentence structures that creates interference with tone.

1 *Focus*

Little or no evidence of a controlling point made about a single topic with a minimal awareness of task and audience.

Content Development

Minimal evidence of content that demonstrates a lack of understanding of the purpose. Superficial, undeveloped writing with little or no support. May be a bare list.

Organization

Little or no evidence of organizational strategies and structures, such as logical order and transitions, which inadequately develop a controlling idea.

Style

Minimal control of language and sentence structures that creates an inconsistent tone.

Persuasive Essays

Persuasive essays are scored using the following rubric:

4 *Focus*

Sharp, distinct controlling point presented as a position and made convincing through a clear, thoughtful, and substantiated argument with evident awareness of task and audience.

Content Development

Substantial, relevant, and illustrative content that demonstrates a clear understanding of the purpose. Thoroughly elaborated argument that includes a clear position consistently supported with precise and relevant evidence. Rhetorical (persuasive) strategies are evident.

Organization

Effective organizational strategies and structures, such as logical order and transitions, to develop a position supported with a purposeful presentation of content.

Style

Precise control of language, stylistic techniques, and sentence structures that creates a consistent and effective tone.

3 *Focus*

Clear controlling point presented as a position and made convincing through a credible and substantiated argument with general awareness of task and audience.

Content Development

Adequate, specific, and/or illustrative content that demonstrates an understanding of the purpose. Sufficiently elaborated argument that includes a clear position supported with some relevant evidence. Rhetorical (persuasive) strategies may be evident.

Organization

Organizational strategies and structures, such as logical order and transitions, to develop a position supported with sufficient presentation of content.

Style

Appropriate control of language, stylistic techniques, and sentence structures that creates a consistent tone.

2 *Focus*

Vague evidence of a controlling point presented as a position that may lack a credible and/or substantiated argument with an inconsistent awareness of task and audience.

Content Development

Inadequate, vague content that demonstrates a weak understanding of the purpose. Insufficiently elaborated argument that includes an underdeveloped position supported with little evidence.

Organization

Inconsistent organizational strategies and structures, such as logical order and transitions, to develop a position with inadequate presentation of content.

Style

Limited control of language and sentence structures that creates interference with tone.

1 *Focus*

Little or no evidence of a controlling point presented as a position that lacks a credible and/ or substantiated argument with minimal awareness of task and audience.

Content Development

Minimal evidence of content that demonstrates a lack of understanding of the purpose. Unelaborated argument that includes an undeveloped position supported with minimal or no evidence.

Organization

Little or no evidence of organizational strategies and structures, such as logical order and transitions, to develop a position with insufficient presentation of content.

Style

Minimal control of language and sentence structures that creates an inconsistent tone.

Sample Essays

Remember the writing prompts you read in the beginning of this lesson? The following are sample four-point responses to these prompts. Notice that the samples clearly respond to the prompt. They contain good opening and closing statements and progress logically from beginning to end. The essays are well-developed and stay focused on the topic throughout. They contain few, if any, errors in usage, sentence construction, and mechanics.

ESSAY WRITING
Lesson 2

Sample Informational Essay

When I think of a special place, I think of my grandmother's house. I have enjoyed visiting my grandmother's house for many years, mainly because it is relaxing, peaceful, and beautiful to me. This is what makes any place special in my opinion.

My grandmother's house is not large. It has a kitchen, a living room, and two small bedrooms, but most people who visit are captivated by its warmth. My grandmother loves to cook, so great smells usually greet you when you walk through the door. She enjoys growing plants and has quite a green thumb. Beautiful hanging planters adorn her windows. In a corner of her kitchen is an antique wicker rocking chair, which is almost always occupied by a friend or family member chatting with Grandma as she cooks. People frequently stop by to visit Grandma. They sit at her kitchen table and sip coffee and make small talk. Grandma is a really good listener.

Since my grandmother lives alone, she only needs one of her two bedrooms. In the second bedroom, my favorite room in her house, she keeps her many books. Except for a small day bed, the room is filled with bookcases and all kinds of books. When she was younger, Grandma was an English teacher. She loves to read and has kept many of the books she has read. When I'm tired or feeling stressed, I like to go in this room and lie on the daybed and read. While Grandma's whole house is special to me, this room is the most special.

In conclusion, I think everyone should have a special place that they enjoy visiting. This place should make them feel relaxed and happy, the way that I feel when I visit my grandmother's house.

Sample Persuasive Essay

Dear School Board:

School field trips should not be canceled for the rest of the school year. I understand how people might mistake a field trip for a mini-vacation from school. Students get to take a break from the monotony of a school day, get on a bus, and travel to a theater, an art museum, a science center, or a historical site. They get to watch plays, see magnificent works of art, try new inventions, or experience life as it was in the past.

What people seem to forget, however, is that these field trips don't allow us to take a vacation from our education. Rather, field trips allow us to enhance what we've learned in the classroom. While books, chalkboards, and lectures are important, hands-on learning gives students the opportunity to take what they have learned in the classroom and see how it is applied in real life. Why silently read a play when you can see it performed live? Why study paintings in a book when you can look at them in person? Why study pictures of the parts of a flower when you can visit a greenhouse and study the real thing?

Field trips provide us not only with a break from the monotony of a regular school day, but a chance to supplement what we learn in the classroom. It would be a mistake to take away this important part of our education simply to save money.

Sincerely,

Josh Greene

POSTTEST

READING

Open-Air Cinemas

Dale Stein

When people go to the movies they are often greeted by long lines at the ticket counter, expensive refreshments, and a sticky floor beneath their feet. One way to skip those aggravations and still enjoy the latest blockbuster hit is to go to a drive-in theater. Back in the late 1940s and 1950s, open-air cinemas, or "ozoners," peaked in popularity. Drive-in theaters were an inexpensive way for families to enjoy a movie in the comfort of their own vehicles. They could load the car with snacks, drinks, and blankets, and settle in for a feature film on a warm summer night. They could talk, joke, and laugh in the privacy of their own car without the fear of being shushed by someone sitting a few rows back.

The first drive-in theater was invented by Richard Hollingshead, a young sales manager from Camden, New Jersey, who wanted to create a way for people to enjoy movies from their cars. He experimented with this idea by mounting a movie projector on the hood of his car and aiming it at a white sheet attached to trees in his yard. Placing a radio behind the sheet for sound, he had the basic ideas for his open-air cinema in place, but Hollingshead strove to make it better. He worried that bad weather might affect the picture, so he used hoses and lawn sprinklers to simulate a rainstorm. The next problem he faced was parking. When one car parked right behind another, the view of the screen was partially blocked. By spacing the cars apart and parking the rear cars on blocks and ramps, Hollingshead discovered a way for all moviegoers to view the screen without a problem. With his idea perfected, Hollingshead obtained a patent for an open-air cinema on May 16, 1933, and less than one month later, he opened the first drive-in theater in Camden. Three large speakers broadcast sound while the screen displayed the picture. The cost for a drive-in movie was twenty-five cents for the car and twenty-five cents for each person.

It didn't take long before other drive-in theaters were built. By 1942, there were about a hundred drive-in theaters across the United States, but World War II slowed this growth. Gasoline, rubber, and metal were all rationed for the war effort, and it wasn't until the war ended that the number of open-air cinemas increased. By 1948, the number of drive-in theaters had risen to 820.

A number of factors contributed to the rising popularity of drive-in theaters, one being the improved technology for sound. Gone were the days of bullhorn speakers mounted to the screen. Instead, drive-in theaters used in-car speakers that allowed moviegoers to adjust the volume to their liking. The baby boom also contributed to the popularity of open-air cinemas. In the years following World War II, mainly the 1940s and 1950s, there was a sharp increase in the number of babies born in the United States. As the number of families with children grew, outdoor cinemas became more family friendly. Theater owners built playgrounds where toddlers and young children could play before the movie started. Some cinemas became small amusement parks offering pony rides, train rides, miniature golf, talent shows, and, of course, refreshments. By the end of the 1940s, open-air cinemas had <u>surpassed</u> indoor cinemas in popularity. They reached their peak in 1958 with more than four thousand outdoor screens showing movies across the country.

Refreshment stands have long been a staple of the drive-in movie industry. Offering a variety of foods from hot dogs, hamburgers, and French fries, to assorted candy and beverages, refreshment stands were often responsible for a large amount of drive-in theaters' profits. In the early days, some outdoor cinemas had "carhops," waiters and waitresses who brought food right to your car window. Other cinemas went with a more traditional cafeteria-style refreshment stand, while some larger theaters offered restaurants with full meals. To increase refreshment sales even more, theaters began showing intermission trailers, or "clocks," between films. These trailers were short, ten- to twenty-minute, animated films featuring dancing snacks and drinks that enticed moviegoers to head to the concession stand. They often had a clock somewhere on the screen counting down the time to the start of the next film.

Just as quickly as they rose to popularity, drive-in theaters began a downward slide. Through the 1960s their numbers remained fairly constant, but the audience changed. Fewer families attended drive-in movies, so cinemas began targeting a teen audience with movies unsuitable for young children. In the 1970s, property values began to increase and many theaters closed to make room for shopping centers. Large indoor theaters offered the newest movies on multiple screens, and outdoor cinemas suffered.

In addition, cable television and videocassette recorders (VCRs) were introduced. These inventions brought Hollywood movies into people's homes. They no longer had to drive to a theater, buy tickets and snacks, and find a place to park. They simply turned on the television or popped in a videotape. By 1983, there were less than three thousand drive-in theaters in the country.

Throughout the 1990s, many open-air cinemas continued to close. Less than six hundred drive-in theaters and 815 screens remained in operation in the United States by 1997. Good news is on the horizon, however. In recent years, some drive-in theaters have reopened, new open-air cinemas have been built, and families are beginning to attend the outdoor pictures once again. These families will treasure the experience as much as those of the past.

1. What was the most profitable aspect of drive-in theaters for those who owned them?

   A fees charged per person

   B fees charged per car load

   C money spent at playgrounds

   D money spent on food and drinks

2. Which statement is an opinion from the passage?

   A By 1983, there were less than three thousand drive-in theaters in the country.

   B These families will treasure the experience as much as those of the past.

   C These trailers were short, ten- to twenty-minute, animated films featuring dancing snacks and drinks that enticed moviegoers to head to the concession stand.

   D To increase refreshment sales even more, theaters began showing intermission trailers, or "clocks," between films.

3. Many people in the 1980s did not visit drive-in theaters because

   A they had a hard time seeing the screen

   B they couldn't hear the bullhorn speakers

   C they didn't want to see children's movies

   D they had videocassette recorders in their homes

4. As used in this passage, what does surpassed mean?

   A upset

   B beaten

   C removed

   D outgrown

5. The main purpose of this passage is to

   A entertain readers with a discussion of drive-in theaters

   B describe what it was like to go to a drive-in theater in the past

   C convince readers that the drive-in theater is making a comeback

   D provide readers with information on the history of the drive-in theater

6. The second paragraph of this passage is mainly about

   A a man's ideas for the first drive-in

   B the man who invented the first drive-in

   C how speakers were used in the first drive-in

   D how a parking was designed in the first drive-in

7. Why did theaters introduce "clocks," also called "trailers" in between films?

   A to sell more advertising

   B to hold people's interest

   C to keep people from leaving

   D to increase refreshment sales

Read this excerpt about a woman who is determined to find out something. Then answer the questions that follow.

Mrs. Rachel Lynde Is Surprised

An Excerpt from *Anne of Green Gables*
by Lucy Maud Montgomery

There are plenty of people in Avonlea and out of it, who can attend closely to their neighbor's business by dint of neglecting their own; but Mrs. Rachel Lynde was one of those capable creatures who can manage their own concerns and those of other folks into the bargain. She was a notable housewife; her work was always done and well done; she "ran" the Sewing Circle, helped run the Sunday-school, and was the strongest prop of the Church Aid Society and Foreign Missions Auxiliary. Yet with all this Mrs. Rachel found abundant time to sit for hours at her kitchen window, knitting "cotton warp" quilts—she had knitted sixteen of them, as Avonlea housekeepers were wont to tell in awed voices—and keeping a sharp eye on the main road that crossed the hollow and wound up the steep red hill beyond . . .

She was sitting there one afternoon in early June. The sun was coming in at the window warm and bright; the orchard on the slope below the house was in a bridal flush of pinky-white bloom, hummed over by a myriad of bees. Thomas Lynde—a meek little man whom Avonlea people called "Rachel Lynde's husband"—was sowing his late turnip seed on the hill field beyond the barn; and Matthew Cuthbert ought to have been sowing his on the big red brook field away over by Green Gables. Mrs. Rachel knew that he ought because she had heard him tell Peter Morrison the evening before in William J. Blair's store over at Carmody that he meant to sow his turnip seed the next afternoon. Peter had asked him, of course, for Matthew Cuthbert had never been known to volunteer information about anything in his whole life.

And yet here was Matthew Cuthbert, at half-past three on the afternoon of a busy day, placidly driving over the hollow and up the hill; more-over, he wore a white collar and his best suit of clothes, which was plain proof that he was going out of Avonlea; and he had the buggy and the sorrel mare, which betokened that he was going a considerable distance. Now, where was Matthew Cuthbert going and why was he going there?

Had it been any other man in Avonlea, Mrs. Rachel, deftly putting this and that together, might have given a pretty good guess as to both questions. But Matthew so rarely went from home that it must be something <u>pressing</u> and unusual which was taking him; he was the shyest man alive and hated to have to go among strangers or to any place where he might have to talk. Matthew, dressed up with a white collar and driving in a buggy, was something that didn't happen often. Mrs. Rachel, ponder as she might, could make nothing of it and her afternoon's enjoyment was spoiled.

"I'll just step over to Green Gables after tea and find out from Marilla where he's gone and why," the worthy woman finally concluded. . . .

Accordingly after tea Mrs. Rachel set out; she had not far to go; the big, rambling, orchard-embowered house where the Cuthberts lived was a scant quarter of a mile up the road from Lynde's Hollow. To be sure, the long lane made it a good deal further. Matthew Cuthbert's father, as shy and silent as his son after him, had got as far away as he possibly could from his fellow men without actually retreating into the woods when he founded his homestead.

Green Gables was built at the furthest edge of his cleared land and there it was to this day, barely visible from the main road along which all the other Avonlea houses were so sociably situated. Mrs. Rachel Lynde did not call living in such a place LIVING at all.

"It's just STAYING, that's what," she said as she stepped along the deep-rutted, grassy lane bordered with wild rose bushes. "It's no wonder Matthew and Marilla are both a little odd, living away back here by themselves. Trees aren't much company, though dear knows if they were there'd be enough of them. I'd ruther look at people. To be sure, they seem contented enough; but then, I suppose, they're used to it . . .

Mrs. Rachel rapped smartly at the kitchen door and stepped in when bidden to do so. The kitchen at Green Gables was a cheerful apartment—or would have been cheerful if it had not been so painfully clean as to give it something of the appearance of an unused parlor. Its windows looked east and west; through the west one, looking out on the back yard, came a flood of mellow June sunlight; but the east one, whence you got a glimpse of the bloom white cherry-trees in the left orchard and nodding, slender birches down in the hollow by the brook, was greened over by a tangle of vines. Here sat Marilla Cuthbert, when she sat at all, always slightly distrustful of sunshine, which seemed to her too dancing and irresponsible a thing for a world which was meant to be taken seriously; and here she sat now, knitting, and the table behind her was laid for supper.

Mrs. Rachel, before she had fairly closed the door, had taken a mental note of everything that was on that table. There were three plates laid, so that Marilla must be expecting some one home with Matthew to tea; but the dishes were every-day dishes and there was only crab-apple preserves and one kind of cake, so that the expected company could not be any particular company. Yet what of Matthew's white collar and the sorrel mare? Mrs. Rachel was getting fairly dizzy with this unusual mystery about quiet, unmysterious Green Gables.

8. What word best describes Mrs. Lynde?

    A busy

    B nosy

    C caring

    D worried

9. As used in this passage, what does the word <u>pressing</u> mean?

    A scary

    B exciting

    C important

    D unnoticed

10. In the last sentence of the fourth passage it says that Mrs. Lynde's "afternoon enjoyment was spoiled." What spoiled her afternoon?

    A She was worried about her neighbor.

    B She could not spend time at her window.

    C She knew she had to visit Marilla Cuthbert.

    D She did not know everything that was going on.

11. This passage is told from the point of view of which character?

    A Marilla

    B Mr. Lynde

    C Mrs. Lynde

    D Someone outside the story

12. What bothers Mrs. Lynde about the kitchen at Green Gables?

    A It is too large.

    B It is too clean.

    C It is old-fashioned.

    D It is surrounded by trees.

13. What is unusual about Matthew Cuthbert's behavior? Use two examples from the passage to support your response.

_____

_____

_____

_____

_____

_____

_____

_____

_____

_____

_____

_____

_____

_____

_____

_____

_____

_____

_____

_____

_____

_____

Read this passage about the way people in ancient China viewed dragons. Then answer the questions that follow.

The Dragons of Ancient China

Throughout history, people all around the world have been fascinated with dragons. There have been thousands of narratives based on the larger-than-life flying lizards and the lionhearted heroes who interact with them. People across the globe find dragons captivating and compelling, but nowhere have dragons ever been as celebrated as in ancient China.

The ancient Chinese perspective regarding dragons is one you may not expect, however. In America, dragons are typically portrayed as menacing and villainous monsters who crush villages, trample castles, and spew fiery breath at any heroes who dare to challenge them. In ancient China, however, the dragons *were* the heroes. These mythical dragons represented every positive characteristic people admired. They were wise, strong, compassionate, and beautiful. In many ways, the *Lung*, or dragon, is a symbol of the nation of China.

The ancient Chinese, from peasants to royalty, believed that the Lungs protected their lands and families and assisted them at all times. In fact, the Chinese believed that the people of their nation were descendants of dragons. They believed that Lungs actually created the Chinese people. The ruling classes and royalty in particular felt a connection to the Lungs. Emperors throughout Asia have claimed to have dragons in their families. For instance, Emperor Hirohito, the leader of Japan from 1926 to 1989, believed that the Dragon King of the Sea created his family 2,500 years ago.

According to myth, dragons not only established the royal families of Asia but also continued to advise them. In the 1200s, a king of Cambodia spent hours at a time locked in a golden tower, supposedly conversing with a nine-headed dragon. The greatest emperors were even thought to be dragons themselves! For centuries, people in Japan were not allowed to observe their emperors. People believed this was because the emperors had transformed into Lungs too glorious to look upon.

Today in America, if someone called you "dragon face," you would probably be highly insulted because the phrase suggests ugliness or meanness. If you lived in ancient China, however, if someone called you "dragon face," you would consider it a great compliment. The phrase "dragon face" would suggest that you were extraordinarily beautiful—like a dragon. In fact, in ancient China anything compared to a dragon was considered beautiful. For example, dragon-house, dragon-throne, and dragon-land would be considered great compliments. According to ancient Chinese tradition, there is even a Year of the Dragon during which great prosperity will come to people, especially those born in that year.

Dragons could be seen everywhere in ancient China. They were carved onto musical instruments because people believed they loved music. They were inscribed on books and tablets, because people believed they had a flair for literature. They were even carved outside of temples because people believed they would protect holy places. Thrones, bridges, and swords were all decorated with dragons. The people of ancient Asia wanted dragons to be involved in all aspects of their lives.

These legendary lizards had appearances just as varied as their tasks. They could have skins of any color of the rainbow, though usually they were green or golden. Some sported horns, wings, gigantic teeth, or even catlike whiskers which would help the dragon move around in the deep, dark oceans. For the most part, dragons' body parts resembled the parts of other animals. Many dragons shared characteristics of animals like bulls, frogs, tigers, eagles, and even camels and rabbits. Some dragons began their lives as carp, a type of fish. Other dragons created unique breeds of animals by mating with the creatures of the earth.

People believed that dragons loved to assist them, but only if people appreciated them. If people were unappreciative, a dragon might cause a flood or a drought to punish them. Because of this, the people of ancient Asia went to great lengths to honor dragons. They even had parades during which people would wear elaborate dragon disguises to celebrate the powerful Lungs. These parades are still held today, which shows the lasting influence of this fascinating Chinese tradition.

14. From the author's point of view, the worldwide appeal of dragon legends is especially interesting because

   A   most legends focus on human characters.

   B   people always realized dragons were imaginary.

   C   the dragons mean different things to different people.

   D   thousands of movies have been made about dragons.

15. What did the body parts of dragons in ancient China usually resemble?

   A   large lizards

   B   other animals

   C   human beings

   D   a type of fish

16. Which **best** describes the organization of this passage?

   A   cause and effect

   B   in order of sequence

   C   compare and contrast

   D   in order of importance

17. Why did the author write this article?

   A   to describe different types of dragons

   B   to persuade readers to think differently about dragons

   C   to entertain readers with a story about dragons

   D   to inform readers about dragons in ancient China

18. People in Japan believed they were not allowed to see their emperors because they

   A   had turned into dragons

   B   were reading about dragons

   C   were spending time with dragons

   D   were drawing pictures of dragons

19. As it is used in this passage, what does the word <u>conversing</u> mean?

   A   talking

   B   looking

   C   showing

   D   changing

20. How did people in ancient China think that dragons influenced their lives? Use two examples from the passage to support your answer.

Read the following poem about daffodils. Then answer the questions that follow.

Daffodils

by William Wordsworth

I wander'd lonely as a cloud
That floats on high o'er vales and hills,
When all at once I saw a crowd,
A host, of golden daffodils;
Beside the lake, beneath the trees,
Fluttering and dancing in the breeze.

Continuous as the stars that shine
And twinkle on the Milky Way,
They stretch'd in never-ending line
Along the margin of a bay:
Ten thousand saw I at a glance,
Tossing their heads in sprightly dance.

The waves beside them danced; but they
Out-did the sparkling waves in glee:
A poet could not but be gay,
In such a jocund company:
I gazed—and gazed—but little thought
What wealth the show to me had brought:

For oft, when on my couch I lie
In vacant or in <u>pensive</u> mood,
They flash upon that inward eye
Which is the bliss of solitude;
And then my heart with pleasure fills,
And dances with the daffodils.

21. Which of the following is an example of personification?

   A "They flash upon that inward eye"

   B "They stretch'd in never-ending line"

   C   "And then my heart with pleasure fills"

   D "Tossing their heads in a sprightly dance"

22. What is the theme of this poem?

   A Cherish happy times.

   B Appreciate the beauty of nature.

   C Remember the good and let go of the bad.

   D Today's experiences can be remembered tomorrow.

23. What is the source of the poet's pleasure in the last stanza of the poem?

   A a sight

   B solitude

   C pictures

   D a memory

24. As it is used in this poem, what does the word <u>pensive</u> mean?

   A angry

   B empty

   C thoughtful

   D disappointed

25. Which of the following is an example of a simile?

   A "I wander'd lonely as a cloud"

   B "A host, a garden of daffodils;"

   C "When all at once I saw a crowd"

   D "Tossing their heads in sprightly dance"

26. This passage is told from which point of view?

   A first-person

   B second-person

   C third-person

   D omniscient

Section 2

Read each of the following passages and answer the questions that follow. You will have 50 minutes to complete this part of the exam. Mark your multiple-choice answers on the answer sheet at the end of this test.
Read the following passage about a woman who worked hard to help Alaska. Then answer the questions that follow.

Margaret Murie, Daughter of Alaska

Margaret Murie was one of the greatest preservationists of the twentieth century. A preservationist is someone who dedicates his or her life to preserving parts of the world, so these places stay clean, healthy, and undisturbed by humankind's often destructive influence.

Murie was born Margaret Mardy on August 18, 1902, in Seattle, Washington. As a young girl she moved to Fairbanks, Alaska, and quickly developed a lifelong love of the Alaskan wilderness. It was there that she began her distinguished career. In 1924 she became the first woman to graduate from the University of Alaska. During this time she also met and married naturalist Olaus Murie who shared her passion for Alaska. The couple even spent their honeymoon on a 550-mile dog-sled expedition!

The Muries soon had children and the family lived together in Alaska, where they became accustomed to taking months-long treks into the wilderness. Olaus worked for the Biological Survey, and, as part of his job, he studied the many plants and animals he observed during these trips. Margaret wrote a book about their unique adventures.

Although their love for Alaska never faded, the Murie family decided to move to Wyoming in 1926. They took up residence in a log cabin and studied the elk of the forests. During that time, they initiated a crusade of letters and lectures to convince the nation's leaders to protect wilderness areas. They didn't want to see nature's splendor disappear under oil rigs or highways or be destroyed by logging companies. Thanks to their efforts, thousands of miles of wilderness areas were designated as wildlife refuge areas, where animals and plants were protected by law.

Though Olaus died in 1963, Margaret, often called Mardy by close friends, continued her efforts to preserve the land that she loved. The next year she joined President Lyndon B. Johnson at the signing of the Wilderness Act, which allowed the National Wilderness Preservation System (NWPS) to select pieces of land in need of protection. As of 1998, the NWPS has been given the task of protecting many millions of acres of land. After this trip, Margaret once again focused her attention on her beloved Alaska. She even spoke before Congress about the importance of keeping Alaska free from exploitation. She believed that the value of Alaska itself was greater than any moneymaking resources like oil or gold that might be found there. She said,

"Beauty is a resource in and of itself. Alaska must be allowed to be Alaska; that is her greatest economy. I hope the United States of America is not so rich that she can afford to let these wildernesses pass by, or so poor she cannot afford to keep them."

Margaret's message hit home, and in 1980, the Alaska Lands Act was passed by President Jimmy Carter. This act greatly expanded the size of the NWPS, America's national parks, and the National Wildlife Refuge System. It promised to keep large sections of land clean and free for future generations to enjoy. Margaret was thrilled and relieved to see these safeguards introduced. She wrote, "when the oil and the minerals have all been found and taken away, the one hundred million acres of national parks and refuges and wild rivers and forests will be the most beneficent treasure in [Alaska]. I would plead with all administrators, 'Please allow Alaska to be different, to be herself, to nourish our souls.'"

In her later years, Margaret dedicated her time not only to societies and councils that watched over America's natural resources but also opened the Teton Science School. Here students of all ages are taught about ecology, which is the relationship between plants and animals and their environment.

In January 1998, Margaret was again summoned by a president. This time it was President Bill Clinton, who awarded her the Medal of Freedom for her dedication to conservation. Clinton said, "We owe much to the life's work of Mardy Murie, a pioneer of the environmental movement, who, with her husband Olaus, helped set the course of American conservation more than seventy years ago." Though Margaret passed away five years later, her contributions live on.

27. What did Margaret do after President Jimmy Carter passed the Alaska Lands Act?

    A   opened a school

    B   moved to Wyoming

    C   took many trips into the wilderness

    D   wrote a book about her adventures

28. As it is used in this passage, what does the word <u>exploitation</u> mean?

    A   progress

    B   movement

    C   development

    D   disappearance

29. What was the main purpose of the Alaska Lands Act?

    A   to map the unexplored wildernesses of Alaska

    B   to compare the wildlife of Alaska to that of Wyoming

    C   to expand the size of national parks and refuges

    D   to honor Margaret Murie for her dedication

30. Margaret Murie would most likely agree that people should

    A   only live in certain areas of the world

    B   turn to other countries for natural resources

    C   consider moving to the wilderness in Alaska

    D   strive to make Alaska look like other states in the U.S.

31. This passage is mainly about a woman who tried to solve problems in Alaska by

    A   raising money

    B   teaching children

    C   fixing things herself

    D   making others aware

32. Write a summary of Margaret Murie's contributions to Alaska. Use at least three details from the passage to support your answer.

> Read this passage about a great archaeological discovery. Then answer the questions that follow.

The Royal Cemetery at Ur

In the 1920s, a team of archaeologists led by Sir Leonard Woolley made an amazing discovery. They excavated an ancient cemetery in what was once Mesopotamia, an area between the Tigris and Euphrates Rivers, most of which is now modern-day Iraq, Kuwait, and Saudi Arabia. The cemetery was located in the ancient Sumerian city-state Ur, which existed over 3,000 years ago. The Sumerians used the cemetery for over five hundred years and it contained about 1,800 bodies and many ancient artifacts. Archaeologists have learned a great deal about the Sumerians and life in ancient times from studying the contents of burial tombs at Ur.

Most people buried in the Royal Cemetery at Ur were common citizens whose funeral rites consisted of merely wrapping their bodies in a reed mat before burial. About sixteen bodies were buried in "royal tombs," large elaborate underground structures with several rooms called chambers. Royal families—kings, queens, and their families—were buried in these tombs. The Sumerians closely intertwined politics and religion and they considered these individuals to be of great importance. Each Sumerian city-state was ruled by a king, who was also a priest. The Sumerians believed that everything around them was controlled by a god. They believed that the sun, moon, and stars were gods. They built magnificent burial chambers for their kings and queens because they thought this would please them.

The Sumerians believed that kings and queens could take things with them on their journey to the afterlife. They filled royal tombs with everything they thought people would need on this journey, including clothes, jewelry, riches, weapons—and even people. It was not uncommon for Sumerian citizens to sacrifice themselves because they believed this would allow them to accompany their king in the afterlife, where they could continue to serve him.

Perhaps the most amazing discovery in the Cemetery at Ur was Queen Puabi's tomb. The queen's tomb was especially valuable because it was discovered intact, meaning it had not been disturbed since the Sumerians closed it thousands of years ago. While Queen Puabi's tomb was built on top of another burial chamber, probably the king's, not much is known about the king, however, because his tomb was *looted*, or robbed, many years ago, probably when the queen was buried.

Queen Puabi's tomb was extraordinary and demonstrated the Sumerians' advanced skills in architectural design. Her body was laid to rest on a table in the middle of an arched chamber in the center of what archaeologists refer to as a death pit. The pit and her burial chamber were filled with exquisite ancient artifacts. Queen Puabi was adorned with an incredible headdress made of gold leaves, ribbons, and strands of beads made from rare stones. She wore a cylinder seal around her neck bearing her name. Her name was carved into the cylinder using cuneiform, the world's first written language, which was invented by the Sumerians. The queen's body was covered in a beaded cape made from precious metals and stone. The cape stretched from her shoulders to her waist. Beautiful rings were carefully placed on each of her fingers.

Members of the queen's "burial party" were discovered in the death pit. Members of this burial party apparently accompanied the queen into her tomb. Each member of the party dressed formally for the special occasion and enjoyed an enormous feast prior to joining Queen Puabi. The burial party included more than a dozen attendants or servants, five armed men, a wooden sled, and a pair of oxen. Four grooms were buried with the oxen, possibly to care for the oxen in the afterlife.

What happened to the members of the burial party to cause their demise? No one is sure, since they died thousands of years ago. However, Sir Woolley and his teams discovered a gold cup near each of their bodies. They suspect that the attendants probably drank poison so they could go to sleep forever with their queen, who may or may not have been already dead.

33. What was special about Queen Puabi's tomb?

    A   It was above a king's tomb.

    B   It contained the queen's body.

    C   It was untouched for many years.

    D   It hidden in a chamber underground.

34. The ancient Sumerians buried their kings and queens in royal tombs filled with treasure because people wanted to

    A   make it to the afterlife

    B   help people in the future

    C   earn the respect of others

    D   treat their kings like gods

35. How were common Sumerian citizens buried in the Royal Cemetery at Ur?

    A   They were buried with their oxen.

    B   They were placed in a large tomb.

    C   They were wrapped in a reed mat.

    D   They were placed in an arched chamber.

36. What was the author's purpose in writing this article?

    A   to explain what it was like to be a Sumerian

    B   to teach readers about Queen Puabi's tomb

    C   to inform readers about an ancient discovery

    D   to convince readers of the Sumerians' greatness

37. You can conclude from this passage that the queen's tomb might have been robbed if

    A   someone was buried on top of her chamber.

    B   her attendants were not buried with her.

    C   her tomb was smaller than the king's tomb.

    D   it had not been discovered by Sir Woolley.

38. What did archaeologists find in Queen Puabi's tomb? Use three examples from the passage to support your answer.

Read this story about a girl who tries to help a stray cat. Then answer the questions that follow.

"Misty"

When Lei first spied a pair of small eyes glowing in the dark near some bushes in her backyard, she darted inside of the screen door on her lanai. But as she peered out, she could vaguely see the outline of a small cat creeping in front of the bushes. Lei opened the backdoor and stepped outside, but the little cat darted into the darkness. Lei considered the cat's presence in her neighborhood strange. She and her mother lived in a wooded area of Englewood, a small town in western Florida, with only a few other houses on their street, and Lei was certain that none of her neighbors owned a cat.

It was drizzling when Lei rose from a restful slumber the next morning, and her first thought was of the little cat she had spied in their backyard the night before. After she ate her breakfast and greeted her mother, she slipped on her raincoat and sandals and headed outside, but she didn't see the cat anywhere. She gently pushed aside the bushes where she had last spotted the cat and looked inside. Crouched down near the bottom bush, the one farthest away from Lei, lay the little cat, damp and dirty, with its paws tucked daintily under its body. Lei longed to reach out to the cat, but the bush the cat was under was out of Lei's reach. Lei noted that the little cat had pretty gray fur and green eyes and that its nose was pushed in further than most other cats' noses. "Are you hungry, sweetheart?" Lei asked. The little cat eyed Lei intently but did not move toward her.

Lei went back into the kitchen and told her mother about the cat. "It's probably a stray, Lei," her mother concluded. Lei explained that she did not think so because the cat looked like some sort of purebred. It didn't resemble the stray cats Lei saw when she and her mother shopped at the wharf, where the shop owners fed dozens of stray cats that seemed to live contentedly among the many people who visited the wharf each day. This cat looked out of place and very scared.

Lei arranged some pieces of lunch meat on an old plate and filled up a bowl with fresh water. She quietly placed the food in front of the bushes and walked back into the house. She watched out of the back window for about a half an hour, but the little cat did not come out of the bushes to eat the food.

Later that day, when Lei returned from her Saturday piano lesson, she glanced out of the back window again. The plate was empty. The little cat must have eaten the food! Lei checked the bushes once again and found the little cat curled up asleep in the same place it had been that morning. It was sleeping so deeply that it did not hear Lei approach, so she quietly returned to her house.

Lei fed the little cat every day during the next few weeks. While the little cat would not confidently approach Lei, Lei would sometimes spy her waiting in front of the bushes in the morning around the time when Lei usually put out her food. Despite her shyness, the cat was becoming more trustful of Lei and would sometimes eat right in front of her. Lei was careful not to touch her (although she desperately wanted to), because she did not want to risk scaring the cat away. The cat's presence in Lei's yard was still a mystery. Lei had called the animal shelters in her area and read the lost and found ads in her newspaper, but no one had lost a cat matching this cat's description. Lei asked her mother if she could keep the little cat.

Mrs. Kim shook her head. "Lei, I know you mean well, and I have no problem with you adopting a kitten or a cat, but I really think you go to a shelter and adopt a cat that you know is healthy and tame. This cat might be feral. That means it might be a wild cat, a cat that hasn't been socialized and isn't tame."

"Oh, I really don't think so," Lei remarked. "I talk to her all the time and she actually listens to me, and she never hisses or swats at me. She's just very scared, that's all. If I can prove to you that this cat is tame and a veterinarian says that she is healthy, will you let me keep her?" Mrs. Kim smiled, and Lei took that as a yes.

Lei's progress with the cat was slow, however. Misty, as Lei had been calling her, was really frightened. While she would stay close to Lei while Lei talked softly to her and would eat her food in front of Lei, she would dart back to her bush if Lei moved abruptly. Lei would not throw in the towel, however. She began moving Misty's food closer to the back door, and Misty hesitantly approached, crouching low to the ground as she moved.

One evening when Lei saw dark clouds approaching, she became concerned about Misty. Before long, the wind had become so strong that the palms in her yard bent in the breeze. Lei glanced at Misty's bush and worried the wind might tear it to pieces. Lei pleaded with her mother to let her leave open the screen door to their lanai, so that Misty could run inside if she had to. Her mother reluctantly agreed, but cautioned that if the storm became too intense, they would have to close the door. Lei and her mother sat at their kitchen table and listened to the pounding rain on the roof of their house. Lei shuddered when thunder clapped hard in the sky and a flash of lightning brightened their back yard. She wanted desperately to check on Misty but knew her mother would never allow her outside in a storm.

When the storm <u>subsided</u>, Lei rose from the table and headed outside. She had tied the lanai door open with string and was relieved to see that the string hadn't broken, but Misty's bush was in bad shape. The wind and rain had pushed it apart and its branches were strewn across the lawn. Panic-stricken, Lei turned her head back toward her mother—but it was Misty she saw, curled up on a lawn chair in the lanai. Lei sighed. Misty had come home at last.

39. Why does Misty come into the lanai?

   A   She wants to find Lei.

   B   She is looking for food.

   C   She is afraid of the storm.

   D   She is eager for company.

40. Why does Lei's mother say she should get a cat from a shelter?

   A   She thinks Misty is afraid of Lei.

   B   She is worried that Misty is not tame.

   C   She knows there are many cats in shelters.

   D   She thinks Misty probably belongs to a neighbor.

41. Lei doesn't think Misty is a stray because

   A   she looks like a purebred.

   B   she likes to be around people.

   C   she has never seen her before.

   D   she does not live at the wharf.

42. As used in this passage, what does the word subsided mean?

   A   calmed down

   B   collapsed

   C   moved along

   D   lifted

43. Which statement is probably true based on the story?

   A   Misty returned to the bush in Lei's yard after the storm.

   B   Misty was actually lost and would one day return to her owner.

   C   Misty decided to live with Lei and her mother.

   D   Misty would be happier living outdoors.

44. Read this sentence from the passage:

   Lei would not throw in the towel, however.

   What type of figurative language is used in this sentence?

   A   a simile

   B   hyperbole

   C   a metaphor

   D   personification

Excerpt from *Incidents in the Life of a Slave Girl*

by Linda Brent

A small shed had been added to my grandmother's house years ago. Some boards were laid across the joists at the top, and between these boards and the roof was a very small garret, never occupied by anything but rats and mice. It was a pent roof, covered with nothing but shingles, according to the southern custom for such buildings. The garret was only nine feet long and seven wide. The highest part was three feet high, and sloped down abruptly to the loose board floor. There was no admission for either light or air. My uncle Phillip, who was a carpenter, had very skillfully made a concealed trap-door, which communicated with the storeroom. He had been doing this while I was waiting in the swamp. The storeroom opened upon a piazza. To this hole I was conveyed as soon as I entered the house. The air was stifling; the darkness total. A bed had been spread on the floor. I could sleep quite comfortably on one side; but the slope was so sudden that I could not turn on the other without hitting the roof. The rats and mice ran over my bed; but I was weary, and I slept such sleep as the wretched may, when a tempest has passed over them. Morning came. I knew it only by the noises I heard; for in my small den day and night were all the same. I suffered for air even more than for light. But I was not comfortless. I heard the voices of my children. There was joy and there was sadness in the sound. It made my tears flow. How I longed to speak to them! I was eager to look on their faces; but there was no hole, no crack, through which I could peep. This continued darkness was oppressive. It seemed horrible to sit or lie in a cramped position day after day, without one gleam of light. Yet I would have chosen this, rather than my lot as a slave, though white people considered it an easy one; and it was so compared with the fate of others. I was never cruelly overworked; I was never lacerated with the whip from head to foot; I was never so beaten and bruised that I could not turn from one side to the other; I never had my heel-strings cut to prevent my running away; I was never chained to a log and forced to drag it about, while I toiled in the fields from morning till night; I was never branded with hot iron, or torn by bloodhounds. On the contrary, I had always been kindly treated, and tenderly cared for, until I came into the hands of Dr. Flint. I had never wished for freedom until then. But though my life in slavery was comparatively <u>devoid</u> of hardships, God pity the woman who is compelled to lead such a life!

My food was passed up to me through the trap-door my uncle had contrived; and my grandmother, my uncle Phillip, and aunt Nancy would seize such opportunities as they could, to mount up there and chat with me at the opening. But of course this was not safe in the daytime. It must all be done in darkness. It was impossible for me to move in an erect position, but I crawled about my den for exercise. One day I hit my head against something, and found it was a gimlet. My uncle had left it sticking there when he made the trap-door. I was as rejoiced as Robinson Crusoe could have been at finding such a treasure. It put a lucky thought into my head. I said to myself, "Now I will have some light. Now I will see my children." I did not dare to begin my work during the day-time, for fear of attracting attention. But I groped round; and having found the side next the street, where I could frequently see my children, I stuck the gimlet in and waited for the evening. I bored three rows of holes, one above another; then I bored out the interstices between. I thus succeeded in making one hole about an inch long and an inch broad. I sat by it till late into the night, to enjoy the little whiff of air that floated in. In the morning I watched for my children. The first person I saw in the street was Dr. Flint. I had a shuddering, superstitious feeling that it was a bad omen. Several familiar faces passed by. At least I heard the merry laugh of children, and presently two sweet little faces were looking up at me, as though they knew I was there, and were conscious of the joy they imparted. How I longed to *tell* them I was there!

45. Who has locked up the narrator?

   A her children
   B Dr. Flint
   C her uncle Phillip
   D her master

46. What is the narrator's biggest problem in the story?

   A She hopes to escape.
   B She is afraid of rats and mice.
   C She wants to see her children.
   D She wants to talk to her grandmother.

47. How does the narrator describe her life as a slave?

   A terrifying
   B very hard
   C not that bad
   D uncomfortable

48. Which of the following is a simile?

   A "It put a lucky thought into my head."
   B "My food was passed up to me through a trap-door my uncle had contrived;"
   C "The air was stifling; the darkness total."
   D "I was as rejoiced as Robinson Crusoe could have been at finding such a treasure."

49. As used in the passage, what does the word devoid mean?

   A hardly
   B without
   C complete
   D occasionally

Read the following passage about popcorn. Then answer the questions that follow.

A *Pop*-ular Kind of Corn

Every weekend, millions of Americans pile into cinemas to see the latest movies. As they enter the theater, they are greeted by the familiar aroma of buttered popcorn. Their noses lure them to the concession stand to buy a bag of the buttery snack. What these anxious moviegoers may not realize as they devour the salty, butter-drenched treat is that popcorn has been a popular snack for centuries.

Archaeologists, scientists who study fossils and artifacts to learn about ancient cultures, have actually studied ancient popcorn. Scientists discovered ancient kernels of popcorn in many parts of the world. The oldest ears of popcorn ever discovered were found in New Mexico's Bat Cave in 1948 and 1950. The ears were believed to be somewhere between three thousand and six thousand years old! Other discoveries have also led scientists to confirm popcorn's old age. Eighty-thousand-year-old fossil corn pollens were found buried beneath what is now Mexico City in Mexico, and ancient popcorn pots made of clay were found in Peru, a country in South America. Christopher Columbus recorded that natives in the West Indies gave popcorn to his sailors when he landed there in 1492. Popcorn was an important source of food for the Aztec Indians of Mexico. They also used popcorn in special ceremonies to honor their gods. Native Americans were planting, harvesting, and eating popcorn long before the Pilgrims arrived in America. But early colonists found a new way to enjoy popcorn—as a breakfast cereal. They served popcorn with sugar and cream.

From the early 1900s to the present, popcorn has been a <u>staple</u> of fairs, carnivals, circuses, and theaters. Even during the Great Depression, when many families were very poor, popcorn remained an affordable treat. During World War II a sugar shortage slowed candy production, but Americans responded by increasing the amount of popcorn they ate. Today, popcorn is still a favorite among many people.

Even though popcorn was an important part of many ancient cultures from different parts of the world, today much of it is grown in the United States. States such as Illinois, Ohio, and Nebraska are known for producing some of the world's best popcorn. Nebraska is even nicknamed the "Cornhusker State." It usually takes about ten days for popcorn plants to emerge from the ground after the seeds are planted. The plant eventually grows to about eight feet tall, and produces ears of corn covered with green husks. Once the plants turn brown and dry, the popcorn is harvested.

Each kernel of popcorn has the potential to become one of those mouth-watering morsels we munch on during a movie. Popcorn kernels are made up of three main parts: the endosperm, the germ, and the pericarp. The endosperm is whitish in color, is made mostly of starch, and surrounds the germ. The germ is

found near the pointy end of a popcorn kernel. The pericarp, also called the hull, is the hard, outer shell. A small amount of moisture is found within the endosperm. When popcorn kernels are heated, the moisture becomes a vapor, much like when you boil water on a stove. But unlike water on the stove, the vapor inside the popcorn kernel is not released into the air, and pressure within the kernel builds as the temperature rises. When the kernel reaches about five hundred degrees, the kernel explodes to release the vapor and turns itself inside out. The white, starchy substance from the center of the kernel is now on the outside, and the hard outer shell becomes the center.

Throughout its history, popcorn has seen many changes in the way it is prepared. Some ancient cultures dropped popcorn kernels into sand heated over a fire. Others had clay pots with legs that stood over the fire allowing the popcorn to be heated. Winnebago Indians cooked popcorn by placing an ear of popcorn on a stick and holding it near a fire, allowing the corn to pop right on the cob! The first mechanical popcorn machine was invented in 1885, and today people use air poppers, microwaves, or stoves to cook popcorn.

50. This passage is mainly about

    A   the history of popcorn

    B   ancient uses for popcorn

    C   how popcorn has changed

    D   different uses for popcorn

51. Which sentence gives the best summary of the article?

    A   Popcorn is often sold at fairs, carnivals, circuses, and theaters.

    B   Popcorn has been enjoyed by many different cultures for thousands of years.

    C   While ancient cultures grew corn, most popcorn today is made from corn grown in the United States.

    D   Native Americans planted, harvested, and ate popcorn even before the Pilgrims arrived in America.

52. What part of a kernel of corn is mostly starch?

    A   the germ

    B   the hull

    C   the pericarp

    D   the endosperm

53. As it used in this passage, what does the word staple mean?

    A   clipped

    B   primary

    C   fastened

    D   essential

54. When is corn harvested from the plant?

    A   when the corn is covered in a green husk

    B   when the plant emerges from the ground

    C   when the plant turns brown and becomes dry

    D   when the plant reaches a height of eight feet

55. How was popcorn cooked in the past? Use two examples from the passage to support your answer.

Read this myth about a famous king. Then answer the questions that follow.

The Myth of King Gilgamesh

Thousands of years ago, the people of ancient Babylonia had great respect for their king, Gilgamesh. He was the son of powerful gods and had superhuman strength. Gilgamesh had keen intelligence and great foresight. He oversaw the construction of Uruk, a beautiful city.

However, Gilgamesh had many flaws. He was arrogant and brash, and frequently neglected the needs of his people in favor of his own desires. He was also oppressive and demanded complete control of everyone in his kingdom. When he began to interfere in people's weddings, the people of Babylonia decided that something had to be done. They flocked to their temple and prayed to their chief god, Anu, pleading with him to confront Gilgamesh and end his exploitation. Their prayers were answered with silence, however, and they left the temple disappointedly.

The next day, a hunter named Shuja headed into the forests outside of the city in search of game. As soon as he stepped into the thick, shadowy woods, he heard the roar of an animal he did not recognize. It resembled a horrifying combination of the growls, hoots, whistles, and barks of a dozen different species. He heard it again, and it was closer this time. Before he could flee, he found himself face-to-face with a hulking wild man surrounded by a team of vicious animals.

An hour later, an exhausted Shuja returned to the city. He looked so ragged and terrified that a crowd gathered around him, inquiring what troubles had befallen him. "I encountered a wild man in the forest training animals for warfare," Shuja explained. "His name was Enkidu, and he said Anu had dispatched him to dethrone King Gilgamesh."

A worried murmur passed through the crowd. *What would happen if such a menacing creature attacked Uruk?* they wondered. The prospect was even less pleasant than living under Gilgamesh's continued oppression. They realized they needed to stop Enkidu, but how could they negotiate with an animal-like man? Some thought they should fight. Others thought they should flee. Still others thought they should surrender to the creature and try to reason with it. Nobody could agree on a course of action.

"Stop this quarrelling. I'll get us out of this predicament," announced Shamhat, one of the most beautiful women in Uruk. The next morning she left the city's protective walls and proceeded into the forest in search of Enkidu. She found him at a watering hole where he and his supporters had stopped to rest. Shamhat approached him confidently, and he could sense that she was not motivated by apprehension or hostility. This caught Enkidu off guard.

Shamhat addressed Enkidu with kindness and compassion, and he responded in a similarly civil manner. They spent the day together and, the next morning, she led him into Uruk as a friend, not an enemy. The people gathered around them and celebrated the <u>cessation</u> of his threat. Enkidu, though disoriented by the new environment, came to love the beauty, companionship, and sophistication he encountered inside the city walls. Taking up residence with some shepherds, Enkidu learned how to behave like a civilized human being.

Meanwhile, Gilgamesh had been having visions of powerful, mysterious newcomers trespassing upon his land. It was therefore no surprise to him to learn of Enkidu's presence in Uruk. Gilgamesh consulted with his mother, who advised him to embrace this newcomer as a friend, because together they were destined for great accomplishments.

What does she know? Gilgamesh thought bitterly. *I would not degrade myself by accepting some wild man as a companion.*

And so Gilgamesh continued his oppression of the people. During a marriage celebration, Gilgamesh interfered again. He was jealous of the groom and intended to kidnap the bride. He believed he was justified in doing so because he was the ruler of Uruk, and he was comfortable with the knowledge that nobody would challenge him.

But he had forgotten about the newcomer, Enkidu, who suddenly appeared in the king's doorway and refused to allow him to break up the wedding.

"How dare you exploit your people for your own gain!" demanded Enkidu.

"How dare you question my decisions!" roared Gilgamesh, lunging forward to attack his challenger.

The two combatants struggled for hours, their powers equally balanced. Finally, Gilgamesh was able to secure an advantage by raising a sword high over Enkidu. Instead of bringing the sword slashing down, however, he paused and then slowly lowered the weapon.

"You are a worthy opponent," he admitted, "and I was wrong to belittle you. I see the wisdom in your challenge, and I will not spoil the wedding." Gilgamesh helped Enkidu to his feet, and they shook hands. "I think my mother was right. If you and I work together, we can accomplish great things for the people of Uruk."

56. Gilgamesh began to respect Enkidu after

    A exploring Enkidu's past

    B deciding to ignore his mother

    C asking the people for their advice

    D learning that Enkidu was a mighty warrior

57. Why were the people of Babylon upset with King Gilgamesh?

    A He forbade them to pray to Anu.

    B He listened to his mother's advice.

    C He made friends with a wild man.

    D He interfered in wedding ceremonies.

58. Why does the author record Gilgamesh's thoughts after he speaks with his mother?

    A to show that Gilgamesh is keeping secrets

    B to explain Gilgamesh's immediate reaction

    C to suggest that Gilgamesh is afraid to speak

    D to contrast Gilgamesh's attitude with his mother's

59. As used in this passage, what does the word <u>cessation</u> mean?

    A end

    B increase

    C meaning

    D alteration

60. Early in the story, Gilgamesh would probably agree with which statement?

    A Might makes right.

    B Mother knows best.

    C Power to the people.

    D All humans are created equal.

61. Why didn't Gilgamesh want to make friends with Enkidu?

    A He was afraid of Enkidu.

    B His mother warned against it.

    C He knew Enkidu wanted to be king.

    D He thought he was better than Enkidu.

62. How did Enkidu change after meeting Shamhat? Use two details from the story in your answer.

WRITING

Session 1

Directions: This part of the writing test contains two passages with multiple-choice questions. Mark your answers on the answer sheet provided at the end of this test.

Passage 1

Read the passage below and answer questions 1–4.

Dear Sophie,

1 I am officialy writing to you from Rome! **2** My family and I left the Newark airport real late last night. **3** The flight was eight and one half hours and we watched a movie. **4** About Italy and everything we can do there. **5** I slept part of the time, and sometimes I just read my book. **6** We landed at dawn, just as the sun was rising. **7** That sun was so bright when it showed through the clouds and into the windows of the plane. **8** It was hot when we stepped off of the plane, and we were very tired, but exctied to be in Italy. **9** At the ariport we took a train to where our hotel was because my mom said it was expensive to taxi. **10** Our hotel is nice. **11** Once we got settled. **12** We went to eat breakfast in our hotel. **13** They did not have eggs or pancakes like we do, but they served a lot of different sweet pastries I was so hungry I ate three.

14 After we took a nap we went to the Pantheon it is a very old temple that probably used to look a lot nicer. **15** We walked around a lot and went to a museum where it was so hot inside that I almost passed out! **16** My brother had fun chasing brids around outside the museum while I bought a bottled water and sat on the big edge of a fountain. **17** After awile I was getting hungry again, so tried to find a restaurant, but no place was making dinner until eight. **18** When it came, I had pizza baked in a wood oven. **19** It was much better then at home and I myself ate the whole thing! **20** The people at the restaurant were nice and kept messing my hair when they walked but I couldn't understand their sayings. **21** After dinner we went to a square and listened to some people playing instruments. **22** Then my brother fell asleep and my Dad had to carry him.

23 Tomorrow we're going to more museums and a place with pony rides. **24** I wish you could see everything hear, but I will rite to you again tomorrow and tell you what we done. **25** Hope your having fun at home and Ill see you soon!

Love,

Lane

1. **Which version shows the correct way to join two sentences for sentence 3?**

   A   The flight was eight and one half hours and we watched a movie about Italy. And everything we can do there.

   B   The flight was eight and one half hours and we watched a movie about Italy and everything we can do there.

   C   The flight was eight and one half hours we watched a movie about Italy and everything we can do there.

   D   While the flight was eight and one half hours. We watched a movie about Italy and everything we can do there.

2. **Which of the following would work best as the concluding sentence for this passage?**

   A   The next day we are going to go shopping for some souvenirs from Italy.

   B   I wish you could see everything here, but I'll write to you again tomorrow and tell you about it.

   C   I am hoping to go to dinner at this place on the water where you ride in a boat to get there.

   D   Traveling in a plane is very exciting at first but after several hours you begin to get restless.

3. **Which word is spelled incorrectly?**

   A   <u>officialy</u> in sentence 1

   B   <u>everything</u> in sentence 4

   C   <u>slept</u> in sentence 5

   D   <u>rising</u> in sentence 6

4. **Which sentences should be joined as one sentence?**

   A   sentences 1 and 2

   B   sentences 3 and 4

   C   sentences 5 and 6

   D   sentences 7 and 8

Passage 2

Read the passage and then answer questions 5–8.

---

1 The school's ecology club is about to begin work on several important projects. **2** These projects will be completed in Melanie Harris Park. **3** We will begin work on Saturday, June 20, and finish on Wednesday, June 24. **4** As you probably know, the Melanie Harris Park is in a state of disarray. **5** It has been neglected for some time now. **6** Ecology Club members plan to work very hard to restore the park, but more help is needed.

7 We need help with projects on each of the following days:

Saturday
8 The Ecology Club will begin by cleaning up garbage on the park's grounds. **9** We will pick up trash. **10** We will cut grass. **11** We will trim bushes.

Sunday
12 Finally, we will plant flowers, vegetables, and native plants. **13** If we get enough help, we would also like to plant native trees in the park.

Monday
14 Many species of birds live in the brush in the park. **15** On Monday, we plan to make birdhouses and nesting boxes to hang in the park. **16** We aim to make the park a beautiful place for birds to live. **17** We will also install a bird bath near the back of the park.

Tuesday
18 On Tuesday, we need help building a compost pile using grass clippings, fruit and vegetable scraps. **19** A compost pile is a type of natural recycling. **20** It will generate important things for the plants in the park.

Wednesday
21 Wear your oldest clothes and bring a paintbrush! **22** We spent our last day in the park painting park benches and the shed near the rear of the park. **23** We have many benches to paint. **24** Be prepared to stay all day. **25** Painting is rewarding work.

---

5. **Which sentence should the writer remove from the passage because it is not relevant to the topic?**

   A   sentence 3

   B   sentence 13

   C   sentence 21

   D   sentence 25

6. In sentence 12, which word best replaces the underlined word?

   A Still

   B Next

   C But

   D However

7. Which sentence would <u>best</u> fit after 17?

   A Birds will fill the park with beautiful music.

   B Last year, a rare bluebird was spotted there.

   C Bird feeders will also be installed near the trees.

   D A bird bath will attract additional birds to the park.

8. Which is the correct form of the verb in sentence 22?

   A We had <u>spent</u> our last day in the park painting park benches and the shed near the rear of the park.

   B We <u>spend</u> our last day in the park painting park benches and the shed near the rear of the park.

   C We <u>spending</u> our last day in the park painting park benches and the shed near the rear of the park.

   D We <u>will spend</u> our last day in the park painting park benches and the shed near the rear of the park.

Session 2

Directions: This part of the writing test contains two passages with multiple-choice questions. Mark your answers on your answer sheet.

Passage 3

Read this passage below and then answer questions 9–12.

> **1** Nellie Bly was the first female investigative reporter. **2** Her first published piece of writing is a letter to the editor. **3** She did not sign the letter but the editor was, so impressed with her writing that he wanted to know who wrote the letter. **4** He saw an ad in the Sunday Paper. **5** Nellie responded to the ad. **6** She came in and introduced herself. **7** Nellie eventually became a reporter, she often went undercover. **8** She wrote articles about people <u>that</u> were treated unfairly.

9. **Which is the correct form of the verb in sentence 2?**

   A   Her first published piece of writing will be a letter to the editor.

   B   Her first published piece of writing was a letter to the editor.

   C   Her first published piece of writing were a letter to the editor.

   D   Her first published piece of writing are a letter to the editor.

10. **Which version shows the correct comma placement for sentence 3?**

   A   She did not sign the letter, but the editor was so impressed with her writing that he wanted to know who wrote the letter.

   B   She did not sign the letter but the editor was so impressed with, her writing that he wanted to know who wrote the letter.

   C   She did not sign the letter but the editor was so impressed with her writing, that he wanted to know who wrote the letter.

   D   She did not sign the letter but the editor was so impressed with her writing that he wanted to know, who wrote the letter.

11. **Which sentence should be divided into two sentences?**

   A   sentence 1

   B   sentence 3

   C   sentence 6

   D   sentence 7

12. In sentence 8, which word <u>best</u> replaces the underlined word?

    A who

    B whom

    C they

    D she

Passage 4

Read this passage below and then answer questions 13–16.

---

1 Ants are truly amazing creatures. **2** Even though it is a very small insect, an _____ legs are very strong. **3** If a person had legs as strong as an ant's leg, the person would be able to run as fast as a horse! **4** An ant can lift twenty times its own body wait. **5** Ants are pretty smart, too, they have many more brain cells than most creatures.

6 Ants also have very strong, scissor-like jaws. **7** They have a great sense of smell and two stomachs! **8** One stomach holds the food an ant will digest itself, <u>so</u> the other stomach holds the food it will share with other ants.

9 But life for an ant isn't all rosy. **10** Ants only live about fifty days—that is, if nothing eats them or steps on them.

---

13. **Choose the correct form of the word to fill in the blank in sentence 2.**

    Even though it is a very small insect, an _____ legs are very strong.

    A   ant

    B   ants

    C   ant's

    D   ants'

14. **Which sentence should be divided into two sentences?**

    A   sentence 2

    B   sentence 3

    C   sentence 5

    D   sentence 10

15. **Which sentence <u>best</u> replaces the underlined word?**

    A   but

    B   and

    C   or

    D   for

16. A word in sentence 4 is used incorrectly. Which change should be made?

A Change <u>twenty</u> to <u>20</u>.

B Change <u>its</u> to <u>it's</u>.

C Change <u>ant</u> to <u>aunt</u>.

D Change <u>wait</u> to <u>weight</u>.

Session 3:   Persuasive Writing Prompt

You will have up to 60 minutes to plan, write, and proofread your response to this writing prompt.

> **Your city council is planning to cut down a century-old oak tree in the middle of the town square to make room for a new movie theater. While the tree is an important part of your town's heritage, the movie theater will bring in needed revenue to the city. Write a letter of your local newspaper editor either for or against cutting down the tree. Use facts and examples to develop your argument.**

Write your essay on the next three pages.

Plan

Before you write:

- Read the prompt carefully so you understand exactly what you are being asked to do.
- Consider topic, task, and audience.
- Think about what you want to write.
- Use scratch paper to organize your thoughts. Use strategies like mapping or outlining.

Write

As you write:

- Maintain a clear and consistent position or claim.
- Include specific details; use examples and reasons to support your ideas.
- Use a variety of well-constructed, complete sentences.
- Use a logical organization with an obvious introduction, body, and conclusion.

Proofread

After you write:

- ❏ Did you support your ideas with specific details?
- ❏ Do the point of view and tone of the essay remain consistent?
- ❏ Check for capitalization, spelling, sentence structure, punctuation, and usage errors.

**PERSUASIVE WRITING PROMPT
FINAL COPY**

If you need additional space, please continue on the next page.

GO ON

USE NO. 2. PENCIL ONLY

PERSUASIVE WRITING PROMPT
FINAL COPY

If you need additional space, please continue on the next page.

GO ON

USE NO. 2. PENCIL ONLY

PERSUASIVE WRITING PROMPT
FINAL COPY

STOP

Session 4: Informational Writing Prompt

You will have up to 60 minutes to plan, write, and proofread your response to this writing prompt.

Write an essay that explains what it means to be a true friend.

Write your essay on the next three pages.

Plan

Before you write:

- Read the prompt carefully so you understand exactly what you are being asked to do.
- Consider topic, task, and audience.
- Think about what you want to write.
- Use scratch paper to organize your thoughts. Use strategies like mapping or outlining.

Write

As you write:

- Maintain a clear and consistent position or claim.
- Include specific details; use examples and reasons to support your ideas.
- Use a variety of well-constructed, complete sentences.
- Use a logical organization with an obvious introduction, body, and conclusion.

Proofread

After you write:

- ❏ Did you support your ideas with specific details?
- ❏ Do the point of view and tone of the essay remain consistent?
- ❏ Check for capitalization, spelling, sentence structure, punctuation, and usage errors.

USE NO. 2. PENCIL ONLY

**INFORMATIONAL WRITING
PROMPT FINAL COPY**

_____

_____

_____

_____

_____

_____

_____

_____

_____

_____

_____

_____

_____

_____

_____

_____

_____

_____

_____

_____

_____

_____

_____

_____

_____

If you need additional space, please continue on the next page.

GO ON ▶

USE NO. 2. PENCIL ONLY

INFORMATIONAL WRITING PROMPT FINAL COPY

_____

_____

_____

_____

_____

_____

_____

_____

_____

_____

_____

_____

_____

_____

_____

_____

_____

_____

_____

_____

_____

_____

_____

_____

_____

If you need additional space, please continue on the next page.

GO ON ▶

USE NO. 2. PENCIL ONLY

**INFORMATIONAL WRITING
PROMPT FINAL COPY**

STOP

Make heavy BLACK marks.
Erase cleanly.
Make no stray marks.

⬤   ◉   ⊘   ⊗   ◖

CORRECT   **INCORRECT**
MARK   **MARK**

Multiple-choice questions

1. Ⓐ   Ⓑ   Ⓒ   Ⓓ
2. Ⓐ   Ⓑ   Ⓒ   Ⓓ
3. Ⓐ   Ⓑ   Ⓒ   Ⓓ
4. Ⓐ   Ⓑ   Ⓒ   Ⓓ
5. Ⓐ   Ⓑ   Ⓒ   Ⓓ
6. Ⓐ   Ⓑ   Ⓒ   Ⓓ
7. Ⓐ   Ⓑ   Ⓒ   Ⓓ
8. Ⓐ   Ⓑ   Ⓒ   Ⓓ
9. Ⓐ   Ⓑ   Ⓒ   Ⓓ
10. Ⓐ   Ⓑ   Ⓒ   Ⓓ
11. Ⓐ   Ⓑ   Ⓒ   Ⓓ
12. Ⓐ   Ⓑ   Ⓒ   Ⓓ
14. Ⓐ   Ⓑ   Ⓒ   Ⓓ
15. Ⓐ   Ⓑ   Ⓒ   Ⓓ

16. Ⓐ   Ⓑ   Ⓒ   Ⓓ
17. Ⓐ   Ⓑ   Ⓒ   Ⓓ
18. Ⓐ   Ⓑ   Ⓒ   Ⓓ
19. Ⓐ   Ⓑ   Ⓒ   Ⓓ
21. Ⓐ   Ⓑ   Ⓒ   Ⓓ
22. Ⓐ   Ⓑ   Ⓒ   Ⓓ
23. Ⓐ   Ⓑ   Ⓒ   Ⓓ
24. Ⓐ   Ⓑ   Ⓒ   Ⓓ
25. Ⓐ   Ⓑ   Ⓒ   Ⓓ
26. Ⓐ   Ⓑ   Ⓒ   Ⓓ
27. Ⓐ   Ⓑ   Ⓒ   Ⓓ
28. Ⓐ   Ⓑ   Ⓒ   Ⓓ
29. Ⓐ   Ⓑ   Ⓒ   Ⓓ
30. Ⓐ   Ⓑ   Ⓒ   Ⓓ

Student Name_____

Multiple-choice questions

31. Ⓐ   Ⓑ   ©   Ⓓ   47. Ⓐ   Ⓑ   ©   Ⓓ

33. Ⓐ   Ⓑ   ©   Ⓓ   48. Ⓐ   Ⓑ   ©   Ⓓ

34. Ⓐ   Ⓑ   ©   Ⓓ   49. Ⓐ   Ⓑ   ©   Ⓓ

35. Ⓐ   Ⓑ   ©   Ⓓ   50. Ⓐ   Ⓑ   ©   Ⓓ

36. Ⓐ   Ⓑ   ©   Ⓓ   51. Ⓐ   Ⓑ   ©   Ⓓ

37. Ⓐ   Ⓑ   ©   Ⓓ   52. Ⓐ   Ⓑ   ©   Ⓓ

39. Ⓐ   Ⓑ   ©   Ⓓ   53. Ⓐ   Ⓑ   ©   Ⓓ

40. Ⓐ   Ⓑ   ©   Ⓓ   54. Ⓐ   Ⓑ   ©   Ⓓ

41. Ⓐ   Ⓑ   ©   Ⓓ   56. Ⓐ   Ⓑ   ©   Ⓓ

42. Ⓐ   Ⓑ   ©   Ⓓ   57. Ⓐ   Ⓑ   ©   Ⓓ

43. Ⓐ   Ⓑ   ©   Ⓓ   58. Ⓐ   Ⓑ   ©   Ⓓ

44. Ⓐ   Ⓑ   ©   Ⓓ   59. Ⓐ   Ⓑ   ©   Ⓓ

45. Ⓐ   Ⓑ   ©   Ⓓ   60. Ⓐ   Ⓑ   ©   Ⓓ

46. Ⓐ   Ⓑ   ©   Ⓓ   61. Ⓐ   Ⓑ   ©   Ⓓ

Make heavy BLACK marks.
Erase cleanly.
Make no stray marks.

⬤   ⊙   ⊘   ⊗   ⬤
CORRECT   INCORRECT
MARK   MARK

Multiple-choice questions

1. Ⓐ   Ⓑ   Ⓒ   Ⓓ   9. Ⓐ   Ⓑ   Ⓒ   Ⓓ

2. Ⓐ   Ⓑ   Ⓒ   Ⓓ   10. Ⓐ   Ⓑ   Ⓒ   Ⓓ

3. Ⓐ   Ⓑ   Ⓒ   Ⓓ   11. Ⓐ   Ⓑ   Ⓒ   Ⓓ

4. Ⓐ   Ⓑ   Ⓒ   Ⓓ   12. Ⓐ   Ⓑ   Ⓒ   Ⓓ

5. Ⓐ   Ⓑ   Ⓒ   Ⓓ   13. Ⓐ   Ⓑ   Ⓒ   Ⓓ

6. Ⓐ   Ⓑ   Ⓒ   Ⓓ   14. Ⓐ   Ⓑ   Ⓒ   Ⓓ

7. Ⓐ   Ⓑ   Ⓒ   Ⓓ   15. Ⓐ   Ⓑ   Ⓒ   Ⓓ

8. Ⓐ   Ⓑ   Ⓒ   Ⓓ   16. Ⓐ   Ⓑ   Ⓒ   Ⓓ

Student Name_____

Posttest Reading Answers

Section 1

1. **D** A.2.3 (make inferences, draw conclusions, and make generalizations)

   The passage says that the concession stands were responsible for a large amount of the profits made by drive-in theaters, so you can conclude that answer choice D, money spent on food and drinks, is the best answer.

2. **B** B.3.1 (interpret and analyze an opinion)

   This question asks you to select an opinion. Remember that an opinion is what someone thinks. Answer choice B, "These families will treasure the experience as much as those of the past," is the author's opinion.

3. **D** A.2.4 (identify and explain the main ideas and relevant details)

   The answer to this question is in the passage. In the 1980s people did not visit drive-in theaters because they had VCRs in their home. You can find this answer in paragraph 7.

4. **B** A.2.1 (identify and apply the meaning of vocabulary)

   When the passage says that drive-in theaters surpassed indoor theaters in popularity, it means drive-ins were more popular. The best choice is B, beaten.

5. **D** A.2.6 (identify and/or describe the author's intended purpose of text)

   While this passage might be entertaining, its main purpose is not to entertain. And while it does mention that drive-ins might be making a comeback, this is not the main purpose. The main purpose of the passage is to provide information. Answer choice D is the best answer.

6. **A** A.2.4 (identify and explain the main ideas and relevant details)

   Most of the second paragraph tells about a man's plans for a drive-in before he received a patent to open it. Therefore, answer choice A is the best answer.

7. **D** A.2.4 (identify and explain the main ideas and relevant details)

   You can find this answer in the fifth paragraph. Drive-ins introduced trailers and dancing drinks and food in between films to increase refreshment sales.

8. **B** B.1.1. (analyze and evaluate characters)

   The beginning of the passage does say that Mrs. Lynde was busy, but she is mostly nosy. She looks out her window watching others and becomes upset because she does not know that Matthew Cuthbert is doing. Answer choice B is the correct answer.

9. **C** A.1.1 (identify and apply the meaning of vocabulary)

   "Pressing" as it is used in this passage means important. Matthew rarely leaves home so Mrs. Lynde thinks that it must be something "pressing" or important.

10.   **D** A.1.3 (make inferences, draw conclusions, and make generalizations based on the text)

The main reason that Mrs. Lynde's afternoon is spoiled is that she does not know where Matthew has gone. This is the best answer.

11.   **D** B.2.2. (identify point of view of the narrator)

This passage is written in the third person. Someone outside of the story tells what is happening.

12.   **B** A.2.4 (identify and explain main ideas and relevant details)

Mrs. Lynde is bothered by the kitchen at Green Gables because it is too clean. She says that it would have been cheerful if it were not painfully clean.

13.   B.1.1 (analyze and evaluate the characters)

Sample answer: Matthew Cuthbert's behavior is unusual because Matthew seldom leaves the house. He is quiet and shy and does not like socializing with strangers. Yet he is driving someplace in the middle of the afternoon workday. His behavior is also unusual because he is dressed up and wearing a white collar.

14.   **C** A.2.4 (identify and explain main ideas and relevant details)

The author seems interested in dragons because they mean different things to different people. Answer choice C is correct.

15.   **B** A.2.4 (identify and explain main ideas and relevant details)

The passage says that the body parts of dragons in ancient China usually resembled other animals, so answer choice B is correct.

16.   **C** B.3.3 (evaluate how the text organization clarifies the meaning)

This passage tells how people in ancient China thought about dragons by comparing them to the way people today think about dragons. The best answer choice is C, compare and contrast.

17.   **D** A.2.6 (identify and/or describe the author's intended purpose of text)

The passage is informational and it gives readers information about dragons in ancient China.

18.   **A** A.2.4 (identify and explain main ideas and relevant details)

This answer is stated in the passage. When people in ancient China were not allowed to see their emperors, they believed it was because their emperors had turned into dragons.

19.   **A** A.2.1 (identify and apply the meaning of vocabulary)

When people conversed with dragons, they talked to them. Answer choice A is the correct answer.

20.   A.2.4 (identify and explain main ideas and relevant details)

Sample answer: In ancient China, people believed that dragons affected almost all aspects of their lives. In fact, they felt that dragons had even founded the Chinese culture. The emperors of China and other parts of Asia felt that they were especially connected to dragons. Some emperors believed they had dragons in their families. Others felt that dragons watched over them and gave them advice. In Japan, people believed that their emperors could even transform into dragons.

Dragons did not only affect Chinese society. They even affected nature. The Chinese believed that dragons lived both high in the sky and deep underwater, and controlled the weather. If a dragon was displeased with the people, it might cause floods or droughts to punish them. There were special dragons in control of the world's major elements: water, earth, fire, wood, and metal. Some dragons even created new types of animals by mating with already existing animals.

The people filled their daily lives with dragons, carving them on temples, swords, musical instruments, and writing tablets. They used the word "dragon" as a great compliment. In order to keep the dragons satisfied, the people held great parades during which they dressed like dragons.

21. **D** B.2.1 (identify and interpret figurative language)

This question asks you to identify an answer choice using personification. The correct answer is A: "Tossing their heads in a sprightly dance." This line gives daffodils human qualities.

22. **B** A.1.4 (identify and explain main ideas and relevant details)

Answer choice B best expresses the theme of the poem. The poet is appreciating the beauty of nature. It is the only answer choice that refers to nature, an important theme of the poem.

23. **D** A.1.4 (identify and explain main ideas and relevant details)

The source of the poet's pleasure in the last stanza is a memory. Answer choice D is the correct answer.

24. **C** A.1.1 (identify and apply the meaning of vocabulary)

The word "pensive" means "thoughtful." The poet says he lies on his couch in a vacant or pensive mood. He implies that these words have opposite meanings. If his mind is vacant, it is empty. "Pensive" would mean the opposite of "vacant."

25. **A** B.2.1 (identify and interpret figurative language)

A simile compares to things or ideas using "like" or "as." Answer choice A is the correct answer.

26. **A** B.2.2 (analyze point of view)

The speaker uses the word "I," so the poem is written in the first person.

27. **A** A.2.4 (identify and explain main ideas and relevant details)

The passage says that after Murie met President Carter, she opened a school.

28. **C** A.2.1 (identify and apply the meaning of vocabulary)

In this sentence, "exploit" means development. Developing land in Alaska is considered a type of exploitation.

29.   **C** A.2.4 (identify and explain main ideas and relevant details)

The passage explains that the purpose of the Alaska Lands Act was to expand the size of national parks and refuges, places that will not be occupied by humans.

30.   **A** A.2.3 (make inferences, draw conclusions, and make generalizations)

This question requires you to analyze what you have read. Murie did not want the entire state of Alaska being developed and felt that some areas should be preserved. Therefore, answer choice A is correct.

31.   **D** A.2.3 (make inferences, draw conclusions, and make generalizations)

Margaret Murie gave many speeches and talked to government officials. She made people aware of the problems in Alaska. Answer choice D is the best answer.

32.   A.2.5 (summarize a nonfictional text)

Sample answer: Although Margaret Murie was not born in Alaska, she moved there as a young girl and loved it for the rest of her life. Many events that shaped her life occurred in Alaska. In 1924, she graduated from the University of Alaska as its first female graduate. She also met her future husband Olaus in Alaska, and they even honeymooned there. Margaret Murie spent nearly her entire life cherishing Alaska's beauty and finding ways to help protect it.

33.   **C** A.2.4 (identify and explain main ideas and relevant details)

The passage says that the queen's tomb was special because it had not been broken into and robbed. Answer choice C is the correct answer.

34.   **D** A.2.3 (make inferences, draw conclusions, and make generalizations)

The passage discusses that the Sumerians closely intertwined politics and religion and that they worshipped many gods. They treated their kings and queens as if they were gods. Answer choice D is the best answer.

35.   **C** A.2.4 (identify and explain main ideas and relevant details)

The answer to this question is in the passage. Common citizens were wrapped in a reed mat and buried. Answer choice C is the correct answer.

36.   **C** A.2.6 (identify and/or describe the author's intended purpose of text)

This question asks you to identify the author's purpose. While answer choice B might seem to be correct, the passage does more than teach readers about Queen Puabi's tomb. It informs readers about the Royal Cemetery at Ur.

37.   **A** A.2.3 (make inferences, draw conclusions, and make generalizations)

The passage says that the king's tomb was looted, most likely when they buried the queen, whose chamber was on top of him. This leads you to conclude that the queen's tomb would have been at great risk of being robbed if another body was buried on top of her chamber. Answer choice A is the best answer.

38.   A.2.4 (identify and explain main ideas and relevant details)

Sample answer: Archaeologists found many things in Queen Puabi's tomb, including a headdress and a cape made of beads. They also found her attendants and a cart and oxen along with an attendant for the oxen.

39.   C A.1.3 (make inferences, draw conclusions, and make generalizations)

Misty comes into the lanai during the storm and Lei leaves the door open for her. You can conclude that the cat came in from the storm because she was afraid.

40.   B A.1.4 (identify and explain main ideas and relevant details)

Lei's mother is worried that Misty is not tame, so she suggests she adopt a cat from a shelter. Answer choice B is correct.

41.   A A.1.4 (identify and explain main ideas and relevant details)

Lei says that she does not think Misty is a stray because she looks like a purebred. Answer choice A is correct.

42.   A A.1.1 (identify and apply the meaning of vocabulary)

When the storm subsided, it calmed down. While answer choice C might also seem correct, we don't know that the storm is completely gone, just that the weather is not as bad. Answer choice A is the best answer.

43.   C A.1.3 (make inferences, draw conclusions, and make generalizations)

The story leads you to believe that Misty will probably live with Lei and her mother after the storm. Answer choice C is the best answer.

44.   C B.2.1 (identify figurative language)

The phrase "throw in the towel" is a metaphor. It means "give up."

Section 3

45.   B A.1.4 (identify and explain main ideas and relevant details)

The narrator's uncle has locked her up to keep her safe from Dr. Flint. Answer choice B is correct.

46.   C B.1.1 (interpret and analyze plot)

Though the narrator complains about the dark, she says that the lack of air is worse. Throughout the passage, the narrator repeatedly wishes to see her children. Answer choice C is correct.

47.   C B.1.1 (interpret and analyze themes)

The narrator says that her life as a slave was not nearly as bad as some. She explains that she was never beaten or harshly treated. Answer choice C is the best answer.

48.   **D**   B.2.1 (identify figurative language)

A simile is a comparison joined by "like" or "as." Answer choice D is correct.

49.   **B**   A.1.1 (identify and apply the meaning of vocabulary)

When the author says her life as a slave with comparatively devoid of hardship, she means that it was generally without hardship. Answer choice B is the correct answer.

50.   **A**   A.2.4 (identify and explain main ideas and relevant details)

Three of the answer choices for this question are supporting details, but the entire passage—the main idea of the passage—is about the history of popcorn.

51.   **B**   A.2.5 (summarize a nonfictional text)

A summary of a passage includes the most important point or points. The best summary is answer choice B.

52.   **D**   A.2.4 (identify and explain main ideas and relevant details)

The endosperm is the part of a kernel of corn that is mostly starch. Answer choice D is the correct answer.

53.   **D**   A.2.1 (identify and apply the meaning of vocabulary)

The word "staple" has several different meanings. In this passage, it does not mean "fastened" or "clipped." The passage says that, since the early 1900s, popcorn has been a staple of fairs, carnivals, circuses, and theaters. While "primary" might also seem to be the correct answer, popcorn is not the primary attraction at these events—but it is an essential part of these events. Answer choice D is the best answer.

54.   **C**   A.2.4 (identify and explain main ideas and relevant details)

The passage says that corn is harvested when the plant become dry and brown. Answer choice C is correct.

55.   A.2.4 (identify and explain main ideas and relevant details)

Sample answer: Some ancient cultures cooked popcorn kernels by dropping them into sand and cooking them over a fire. Others heated popcorn in clay pots, which they placed over a fire. The Winnebago Indians cooked popcorn by letting it pop right on the cob.

56.   **D**   A.1.4 (identify and explain main ideas and relevant details)

Gilgamesh began to respect Enkido after he fought him. Answer choice D is correct.

57.   **D**   B.1.1 (interpret and analyze plot)

King Gilgamesh had his ups and downs, but the biggest problem he caused the people of Babylon was that he interfered in wedding ceremonies. The story said he felt justified in kidnapping brides because he was the king and nobody could stop him.

58.   **D**   A.2.6 (identify and/or describe the author's intended purpose of text)

The author records Gilgamesh's thoughts to show that he does not agree with his mother.

59.   **A**   A.1.1 (identify and apply the meaning of vocabulary)

This question asks you about the vocabulary word cessation. "Cessation" means "end." The sentence and the paragraph it came from told about how Enkidu stopped being a fearsome menace to the people of Uruk. When that happened, they were glad because of the cessation, or end, of his threat.

60. **A** B.1.1 (interpret and analyze characters)

In the beginning of the story, Gilgamesh rules with his might. Answer choice A is the best answer.

61. **D** B.1.1 (interpret and analyze characters)

Gilgamesh thought he was much better than Enkidu. This is why he did not want to be friends with him. Answer choice D is correct.

62. B.1.1 (interpret and analyze characters)

Sample answer: Shamhat took a unique approach to dealing with Enkidu. The other citizens of Uruk reacted to him with fear and anger. Shuja tried to run away from him. Other citizens wanted to attack him, or surrender to him. Shamhat chose to approach him with kindness and respect. Enkidu didn't expect this treatment and it warmed his heart. He returned Shamhat's civil attitude and became a friend of Uruk.

Posttest Writing Answers

Session 1

1. **B** 1.5.8.F (edit writing using the conventions of language)

The only answer choice that correctly eliminates the sentence fragment is answer choice B.

2. **B** 1.5.8.E (revise writing after rethinking logic of organization and rechecking central idea)

Answer choice B is the best conclusion because it signals the end of the letter.

3. **A** 1.5.8.F (edit writing using the conventions of language)

The word "officialy" is spelled "officially."

4. **B** 1.5.8.F (edit writing using the conventions of language)

Sentence 4 is actually a phrase, so the two "sentences" should be combined to form one sentence.

5. **D** 1.5.8.E (revise writing after rethinking logic of organization and rechecking central idea)

The last sentence of this passage has nothing to do with fixing up the park.

6. **B** 1.5.8.E (revise writing after rethinking logic of organization and rechecking central idea)

"Finally" doesn't work because the writer isn't finished discussing what they will do during the clean-up. Answer choice B is the best answer.

7. **D** 1.5.8.E (revise writing after rethinking logic of organization and rechecking central idea)

Sentence 17 is about a bird bath. You should choose the sentence that best fits this idea.

8. **D** 1.5.8.F (edit writing using the conventions of language)

The writer should use the future tense, since the activities being discussed did not happen yet.

Session 2

9. **B** 1.5.8.F (edit writing using the conventions of language)

"Was" is the correct answer because Nellie wrote the letter a very long time ago.

10. **A** 1.5.8.F (edit writing using the conventions of language)

A comma should be placed before the coordinating conjunction.

11. **D** 1.5.8.F (edit writing using the conventions of language)

Sentence 7 is really two sentences; it contains two complete thoughts.

12. **A** 1.5.8.E (revise writing after rethinking logic of organization and rechecking central idea)

"Who" is the correct pronoun in this sentence. If you weren't sure you could find the correct answer using process of elimination.

13. **C** 1.5.8.F (edit writing using the conventions of language)

Answer choice C is correct; you need to make "ant" possessive.

14. **C** 1.5.8.F (edit writing using the conventions of language)

Sentence 5 is really two sentences. An easy way to divide them is to put a period after the word "too."

15. **B** 1.5.8.E (revise writing after rethinking logic of organization and rechecking central idea)

"And" is the best way to join these sentences.

16. **D** 1.5.8.E (revise writing after rethinking logic of organization and rechecking central idea)

"Weight" is the correct word here, since the author is discussing how much an ant can lift.

Session 3

Sample 4-point essay:

To the City Council:

I have just learned of your plans to cut down the oak tree in the center of town square. The thought of losing another historical landmark of our town saddens me. The old oak tree has been a part of so many lives. When my great-grandparents got married, they were photographed under the old oak. We have pictures of my grandmother and grandfather as toddlers swinging from the branches. They too were photographed there on their wedding day, as were my parents. On my bedroom wall, I have a photograph of my best friend and me attempting to climb the massive tree when we were barely old enough to walk. Obviously, this tree has been around for many generations, and I always hoped that one day my own children would get to experience the joy of sitting under the old oak on a hot, summer day.

I understand that one reason given for the removal of the tree is that the branches might impede the poles and wires. It's never been a problem for city workers to trim these branches before. Why is it a problem now? I think the bigger issue is that you want to build a movie theater to bring in more money. The last thing this town needs is another movie theater. We already have a cinema at each end of town. Is it really necessary to add another? These massive buildings, with their long lines and gaudy lights, detract from the natural beauty of our town. Why destroy the one glorious work of nature we have left? I urge you to think very carefully before you plow under another historical landmark.

Persuasive Essays

Persuasive essays are scored using the following rubric:

4   Focus

Sharp, distinct controlling point presented as a position and made convincing through a clear, thoughtful, and substantiated argument with evident awareness of task and audience.

Content Development

Substantial, relevant, and illustrative content that demonstrates a clear understanding of the purpose. Thoroughly elaborated argument that includes a clear position consistently supported with precise and relevant evidence. Rhetorical (persuasive) strategies are evident.

Organization

Effective organizational strategies and structures, such as logical order and transitions, to develop a position supported with a purposeful presentation of content.

Style

Precise control of language, stylistic techniques, and sentence structures that creates a consistent and effective tone.

3   Focus

Clear controlling point presented as a position and made convincing through a credible and substantiated argument with general awareness of task and audience.

Content Development

Adequate, specific, and/or illustrative content that demonstrates an understanding of the purpose. Sufficiently elaborated argument that includes a clear position supported with some relevant evidence. Rhetorical (persuasive) strategies may be evident.

Organization

Organizational strategies and structures, such as logical order and transitions, to develop a position supported with sufficient presentation of content.

Style

Appropriate control of language, stylistic techniques, and sentence structures that creates a consistent tone.

2   Focus

Vague evidence of a controlling point presented as a position that may lack a credible and/or substantiated argument with an inconsistent awareness of task and audience.

Content Development

Inadequate, vague content that demonstrates a weak understanding of the purpose. Insufficiently elaborated argument that includes an underdeveloped position supported with little evidence.

Organization

Inconsistent organizational strategies and structures, such as logical order and transitions, to develop a position with inadequate presentation of content.

Style

Limited control of language and sentence structures that creates interference with tone.

1   Focus

Little or no evidence of a controlling point presented as a position that lacks a credible and/or substantiated argument with minimal awareness of task and audience.

Content Development

Minimal evidence of content that demonstrates a lack of understanding of the purpose. Unelaborated argument that includes an undeveloped position supported with minimal or no evidence.

Organization

Little or no evidence of organizational strategies and structures, such as logical order and transitions, to develop a position with insufficient presentation of content.

Style

Minimal control of language and sentence structures that creates an inconsistent tone.

Session 4

Sample 4-point essay:

A true or real friend should be honest, loyal, and trustworthy. These are the most important traits in a friend. While I consider many people friends, like most people, I have only a few true friends.

Honesty is a very important trait in a friend. Suppose you are dressed to go out and you are wearing something you think looks good on you—but it really doesn't. A true friend will tell you to change. My friend Lisa is a true friend. Lisa is honest with me, but she criticizes in a gentle way. When I liked a boy and he didn't really like me, Lisa told me the truth, not just what I wanted to hear.

Loyalty is also very important. A true friend will stick with you even when you make a fool out of yourself. Last year, when I was walking down the steps to enter the school cafeteria, I slipped and fell. Well, I was more embarrassed than hurt. Lots of people laughed. But my friends Lisa and Tina did not laugh. They simply helped me up and were more concerned with whether or not I was hurt than what others thought. They are true friends.

Lastly, true friends can be trusted. They will not say bad things about you behind your back. If they have a problem with something you have done, they will tell you about it instead of talking about you to other people. You know that your true friends would not intentionally do anything to hurt you. That is the beauty of having a true friend.

Informational Essays

Informational essays are scored using the following rubric:

4   Focus

Sharp, distinct controlling point made about a single topic with evident awareness of task and audience.

Content Development

Substantial, relevant, and illustrative content that demonstrates a clear understanding of the purpose. Thorough elaboration with effectively presented information consistently supported with well-chosen details.

Organization

Effective organizational strategies and structures, such as logical order and transitions, which develop a controlling idea.

Style

Precise control of language, stylistic techniques, and sentence structures that creates a consistent and effective tone.

3   Focus

Clear controlling point made about a single topic with general awareness of task and audience.

Content Development

Adequate, specific, and/or illustrative content that demonstrates an understanding of the purpose. Sufficient elaboration with clearly presented information supported with well-chosen details.

Organization

Organizational strategies and structures, such as logical order and transitions, which develop a controlling idea.

Style

Appropriate control of language, stylistic techniques, and sentence structures that creates a consistent tone.

2 Focus

Vague evidence of a controlling point made about a single topic with an inconsistent awareness of task and audience.

Content Development

Inadequate, vague content that demonstrates a weak understanding of the purpose. Underdeveloped and/or repetitive elaboration with inconsistently supported information. May be an extended list.

Organization

Inconsistent organizational strategies and structures, such as logical order and transitions, which ineffectively develop a controlling idea.

Style

Limited control of language and sentence structures that creates interference with tone.

1 Focus

Little or no evidence of a controlling point made about a single topic with a minimal awareness of task and audience.

Content Development

Minimal evidence of content that demonstrates a lack of understanding of the purpose. Superficial, undeveloped writing with little or no support. May be a bare list.

Organization

Little or no evidence of organizational strategies and structures, such as logical order and transitions, which inadequately develop a controlling idea.

Style

Minimal control of language and sentence structures that creates an inconsistent tone.